Essential algorithms for A level Computer Science

D Hillyard

C Sargent

Published by
CRAIGNDAVE LTD
12 Tweenbrook Avenue
Gloucester
Gloucestershire
GL1 5JY
United Kingdom
admin@craigndave.co.uk
www.craigndave.org
2018

Craig 'n' Dave

Every effort has been made to trace copyright holders and to obtain their permission for the use of copyrighted material. We apologise if any have been overlooked. The authors and publisher will gladly receive information enabling them to rectify any reference or credit in future editions.

Front cover artwork: the binary tree created using https://www.visnos.com/demos/fractal

Text © D.Hillyard and C.Sargent 2018
Original illustrations © D.Hillyard and C.Sargent 2018
Edited by A.Fenn
Graphics and typesetting by CRAIGNDAVE LTD
First edition 2018

ISBN: 978-1-7943594-2-0

Copyright © D.Hillyard and C.Sargent 2018

A copy of this book is held in the British library

All rights reserved.
No part of this publication may be reproduced, stored in a retrieval system, or transmitted in any form or by any means without the prior written permission of the copyright owner.

About the authors

David Hillyard

David is a post-graduate qualified teacher with a Bachelor of Science (Honours) in Computing with Business Information Technology. David has twenty years' teaching experience in ICT and computing in three large comprehensive schools in Cheltenham, Gloucestershire. He is an assistant headteacher, former head of department, chair of governors and founding member of a multi-academy trust of primary schools.

Formerly subject leader for the Gloucestershire Initial Teacher Education Partnership (GITEP) at the University of Gloucestershire, David has successfully led a team of PGCE/GTP mentors across the county.

His industry experience includes programming for the Ministry of Defence. A self-taught programmer, he wrote his first computer game at ten years old.

Craig Sargent

Craig is a post-graduate qualified teacher with a Bachelor of Science (Honours) in Computer Science with Geography. Craig has fourteen years' teaching experience in ICT and computing in a large comprehensive school in Stroud, Gloucestershire and as a private tutor. A head of department, examiner and moderator for awarding bodies in England, Craig has authored many teaching resources for major publishers.

He also previously held roles as a Computing at School (CAS) Master Teacher and regional coordinator for the Computing Network of Excellence.

His industry experience includes freelance contracting for a large high street bank and programming for the Ministry of Defence. He also wrote his first computer game in primary school.

Preface

The aim of this book is to provide students and teachers of A level Computer Science with a comprehensive guide to the algorithms students need to understand for examinations. Each chapter examines a data structure or algorithm and includes an explanation of how it works, real-world applications, a step-by-step example, pseudocode, actual code in two languages and a description of the space and time complexity.

Coded solutions are provided in Python 3 because it is the most popular language taught at GCSE, though we also provide them in Visual Basic Console (2015 onwards) because it most closely resembles pseudocode and coded examples that students will need to work with in examinations. These coded solutions can be downloaded from craigndave.org/product/algorithms.

Additional material to support this book is available at craigndave.org/algorithms.

For those students studying other languages such as C++/C# or Java, it would be a great exercise to translate the code presented in this book into those languages.

Each chapter has been carefully considered to ensure it matches the needs of students and the requirements of examining bodies without being unnecessarily complex. Wherever possible, a consistent approach has been adopted to make it easier to see how algorithms expressed in English and pseudocode relate to real coded solutions. Therefore, some conventions have been adopted:

- ++ += -= for incrementing and decrementing variables has been avoided, instead favouring x = x +1.
- Swapping of variables using approaches such as a, b = b, a. A three-way swap with a temporary variable is favoured in examinations.
- The fewest functions or methods as possible to achieve a solution.

The result is not necessarily the most efficient code but an implementation that is most suitable for the level of study.

There are many ways to code these algorithms. Taking the depth-first search as an example, it can be coded using iteration or recursion, with a dictionary, objects or arrays. That is six different implementations, but even these are not exhaustive. When combined with a programmer's own approach and the available commands in the language, the number of possibilities for coding these algorithms is huge. It is important that students recognise the underlying data structures, understand the way an algorithm works and can determine the output from a piece of code. Therefore, the approaches and solutions presented in this book are one solution, not the only solution.

Examination board mapping

	OCR GCSE (J276)	OCR GCE AS Level (H046)	OCR GCE A Level (H446)	AQA GCSE (8520)	AQA GCE AS Level (7516)	AQA GCE A Level (7517)	WJEC GCSE (C00/1157/9)	WJEC GCE AS Level (601/5391/X)	WJEC GCE A Level (601/5345/3)	Cambridge IGCSE (0984)	Pearson GCSE & IGCSE (1CP1) (4CP0)	Pearson BTEC Nationals (603/0446/7) (601/7341/5) (601/7343/9) (603/0445/5) (601/7342/7)	Pearson BTEC Higher Nationals (603/0472/8) (603/0471/6)
Sorting algorithms													
Bubble sort	✓	✓	✓	✓		✓	✓	✓	✓		✓	✓	
Insertion sort	✓	✓	✓					✓	✓			✓	✓
Merge sort	✓		✓	✓		✓		✓	✓		✓		✓
Quick sort			✓						✓			✓	✓
Searching algorithms													
A* algorithm			✓										✓
Binary search	✓	✓	✓	✓		✓	✓	✓	✓				✓
Dijkstra's shortest path			✓			✓			✓				✓
Linear search	✓	✓	✓	✓		✓	✓	✓	✓		✓	✓	✓
Data structure algorithms													
Arrays	✓	✓	✓	✓	✓	✓	✓	✓	✓	✓	✓	✓	✓
Dictionaries						✓							
Graphs			✓			✓							
Hash tables			✓			✓			✓				✓
Linked lists			✓						✓				✓
Lists	✓	✓	✓						✓		✓	✓	✓
Queues		✓	✓			✓			✓			✓	✓
Stacks		✓	✓		✓	✓			✓			✓	✓
Trees / Binary trees			✓			✓			✓				✓

Contents

FUNDAMENTAL DATA STRUCTURES — 1

Array	2
Dictionary	6
List	10
In summary	13

HIGHER ORDER DATA STRUCTURES — 14

Binary Tree	15
Graph	38
Linked list	69
Queue	79
Stack	87
In summary	95

SEARCHING ALGORITHMS — 96

Binary search	97
Hash table search	103
Linear search	112
In summary	117

SORTING ALGORITHMS — 118

Bubble sort	119
Insertion sort	124
Merge sort	129
Quicksort	139
In summary	152

OPTIMISATION ALGORITHMS — 154

Dijkstra's shortest path	155
A* pathfinding	169
In summary	181

FUNDAMENTAL DATA STRUCTURES

A feature of imperative programming languages, these abstractions of memory allow for the creation of higher order data structures.

Essential algorithms for A level Computer Science

Array

| OCR AS Level | OCR A Level | AQA AS Level | AQA A Level |
| WJEC AS Level | WJEC A Level | BTEC Nationals | BTEC Highers |

An array is a collection of items (called **elements**) of the same data type. An array is used to hold a collection of data that would otherwise be stored in multiple variables. For example, to store the names of four people, you could have four variables: name1, name2, name3 and name4. The problem with this approach is that it would not be possible to refer to a specific name or loop through all the names with a for or while command. That is because the number or index is part of the identifier (name of the variable). Instead, we need to declare name1 as name[1] and so on. Note how the index is now enclosed in brackets. Some programming languages used curved brackets while others use square brackets.

Assigning data to the array can be done using syntax similar to:

```
name[0] = "Craig"
name[1] = "Dave"
name[2] = "Sam"
name[3] = "Carol"
```

Notice with four names, the maximum index is 3. That is because arrays are usually zero-indexed – i.e., the first item is stored at index zero. It is not necessary to do this; you could start at index 1, but why waste memory unnecessarily?

Now it is possible to use an iteration to output all the data in the array:

```
For index = 0 to 3         → For loop
    Print(name[index])
Next
```

This is an extremely useful algorithm that you need to understand at all levels of study. The alternative code would be:

```
Print(name1)
Print(name2)
Print(name3)
Print(name4)
```

It is a misconception that using an array instead of individual variables is more memory-efficient. The same amount of data still needs to be stored, but an array makes the algorithm **scalable**. That means we only need to change the number 3 in the iteration to change the number of names output. You can see how implementing code with a thousand names without an iteration would not only be time-consuming but also impractical.

There are two limitations of using arrays.

1. All the data elements of an array must contain the same data type. For example, an array of strings cannot contain an integer.

2. The size of an array is determined when it is declared – i.e., when the algorithm is written – and cannot be changed when the program is running. This is known as a static data structure.

Arrays can be declared larger than they need to be so that data can be inserted into an empty index later. This is the case when implementing stacks, queues and trees using arrays. It is not memory-efficient, and you would need to use either a search or a variable called a pointer to keep track of the last item in the structure.

The static restriction of arrays is due to memory needing to be allocated for the data. An index register is used by the CPU to store the index of an array to be accessed, and by incrementing this register, you can

2

access the next item in the array. Therefore, all items in an array must occupy a contiguous memory space in RAM in what is called the heap, a place in memory where data structures are stored.

Modern programming languages allow for the re-declaration of the size of an array at run-time. They do this by finding a new place in the heap for the entire data structure and moving it to that location. Therefore, the lines are somewhat blurred between arrays being static or dynamic data structures. During examinations, you should always assume arrays to be static.

Arrays may have multiple indexes in what is known as a multi-dimension array. An array of two dimensions is referred to as a two-dimensional array. By using two dimensions, we can store a grid of data.

Applications of an array

Arrays are used in situations where you have many related data items that require the same data type, to be accessed either by an index or a searching algorithm. Not all programming languages support arrays, and lists have become a popular alternative due to their dynamic use of memory.

Operations on an array

Typical operations that can be performed on an array include:

- Lookup: return an element from an index
- Assign: set the element for a given index
- Re-declare: change the size of the array at run-time (not universally supported)
- Linear search: finding an element in the array

Craig'n'Dave videos

https://www.craigndave.org/algorithm-array

Did you know?

A vector is another type of data structure that shares the properties of both arrays and lists. It is considered to be a dynamic array that can change size at run-time. A vector can store different data types, including any type of object, although it uses contiguous memory like an array.

Essential algorithms for A level Computer Science

An array illustrated

One-dimensional array	Two-dimensional array

One-dimensional array

Name

Index	Element
3	Carol
2	Sam
1	Dave
0	Craig

Name[2] = Sam

Two-dimensional array

Board

Index	0	1	2
0	O	X	
1		O	
2			X

Board[1,0] = "X"

Notice that in the example of the two-dimensional array, the first index was chosen to represent the x position in the grid and the second index represents the y position. This is a useful approach when representing game-boards in memory, but it is not necessary. It is acceptable for the first index to represent the y position and the second index to represent the x position. In memory, the grid doesn't exist at all. Indexes are simply memory addresses, so the structure itself is abstracted. It is up to the programmer how they visualise the data structure in their own mind.

💡 Did you know?

Two-dimensional arrays are sometimes called matrices. John von Neumann wrote the first array sorting program — the "merge sort" — in 1945 while building the first stored-program computer. All the other data structures can be created using arrays.

Efficiency of an array

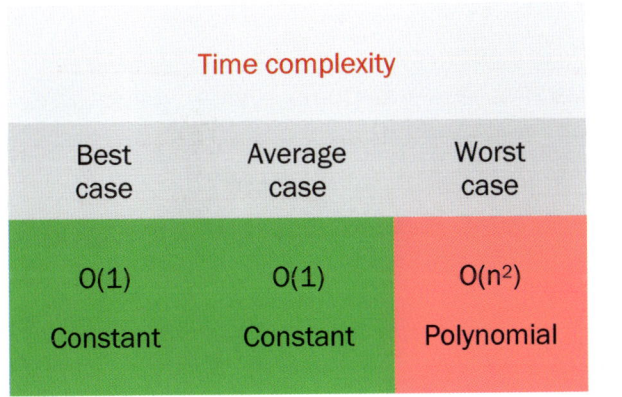

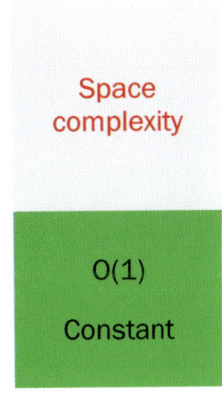

	Time complexity		Space complexity
Best case	Average case	Worst case	
O(1) Constant	O(1) Constant	O(n²) Polynomial	O(1) Constant

Since an array is considered a static data structure, its memory footprint is always known at run-time and, therefore, it has a constant space complexity of O(1).

Calculating the time complexity with an array is dependent on the algorithms being implemented with it. Simply assigning or returning an element from an index can be done immediately without searching through the array — so, at best, it has a constant time complexity of O(1).

However, when implementing a linear search on an array, the average time complexity becomes linear: O(n). Meanwhile, a binary search becomes logarithmic: O(log n). With multi-dimensional arrays, if a nested loop is required to iterate over all the elements, it becomes polynomial: O(n²). The exponent represents the number of dimensions in the structure. In the case of a three-dimensional array it would be O(n³).

Did you know?

A string is actually an array of characters. In many programming languages, you can use an index to access an individual character within a string.

Essential algorithms for A level Computer Science

Dictionary

A dictionary is a data structure used for storing related data. It is often referred to as an associative array, as it stores two sets of data that are associated with each other by mapping keys to values. It is also known as a key-value pair or hashmap. A dictionary is an implementation of a hash table search but is usually a fundamental data type in high-level languages. Instead of a programmer having to code a hash table search, high-level languages provide the dictionary data type within the language. The single value in a key-value pair can also be a list of items, making this a very versatile data structure for a programmer.

Applications of a dictionary

Dictionaries are used as an extremely efficient alternative to searching algorithms. They are also suitable for databases. For example, NoSQL — an acronym for "not only SQL" — makes extensive use of dictionaries. Symbol tables in the syntax analysis stage of compilation make use of dictionaries, as do dictionary encoding compression algorithms. Objects in JavaScript and JSON, a data-interchange standard also make use of the data structure. Dictionaries are also ideal for implementing depth and breadth-first searching algorithms with graph data structures, and are useful in any situation where an efficient value look-up or search is required like telephone numbers in contact lists.

Operations on a dictionary

Typical operations that can be performed on a dictionary include:

- Add key/value: adding a new key value pair to the dictionary
- Remove key/value: removing a key value pair from the dictionary
- Lookup: return the value from a key

Craig'n'Dave video

https://www.craigndave.org/algorithm-dictionary

Dictionary search in simple-structured English

1. Read a key
2. Lookup key in dictionary
3. If the key exists, return the matching value; if not, return an error

Fundamental data structures

Dictionary illustrated

If illustrations help you remember, this is how you can picture a dictionary:

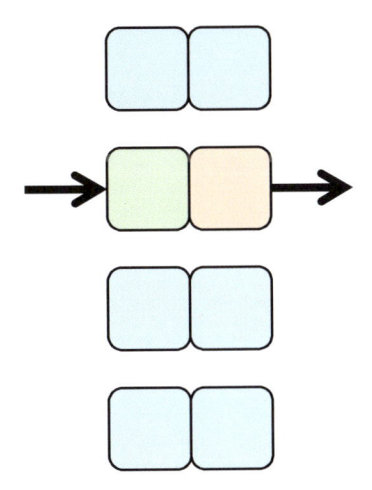

Example of a dictionary search

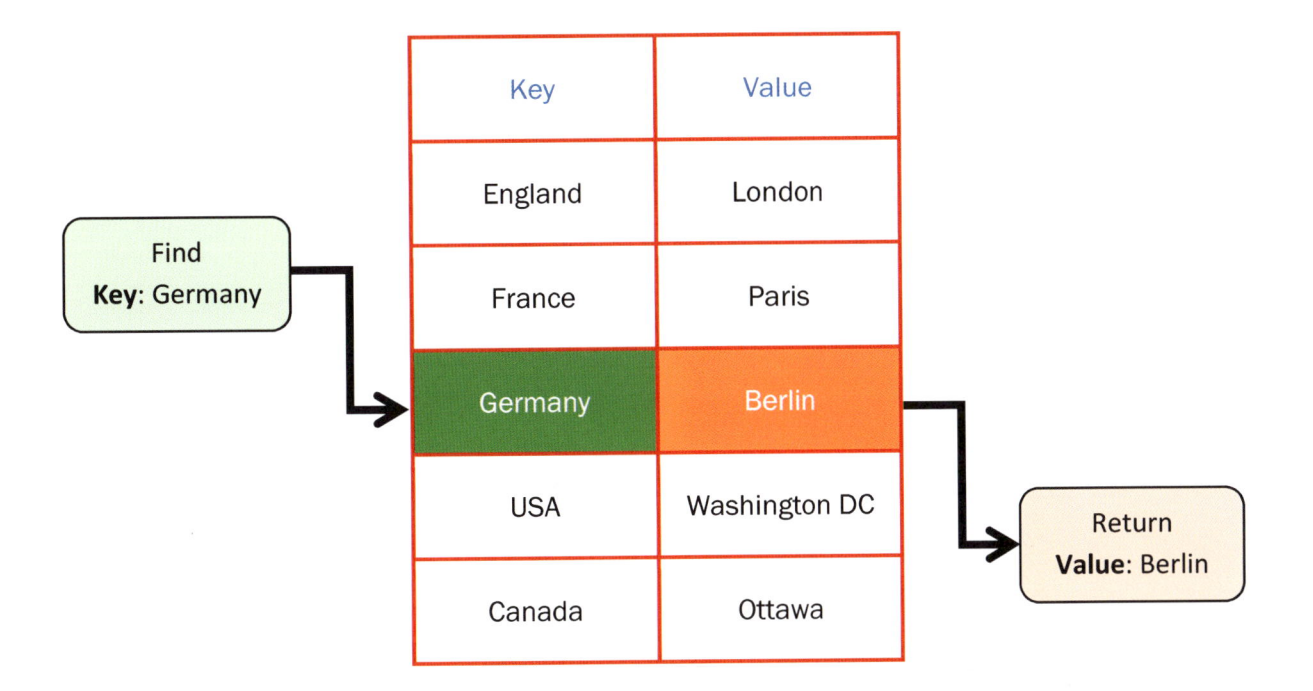

Key	Value
England	London
France	Paris
Germany	Berlin
USA	Washington DC
Canada	Ottawa

Find
Key: Germany

Return
Value: Berlin

7

Essential algorithms for A level Computer Science

Pseudocode for a dictionary search

```
key = input("Enter the key: ")
If key in dictionary Then
        Return dictionary[key].value
Else
        Return "Not found"
End If
```

Dictionary search coded in Python

```python
dictionary = {"England":"London","France":"Paris","Germany":"Berlin"}
key = input("Enter the key: ")
if key in dictionary:
    print(dictionary[key])
else:
    print("Not found")
```

Dictionary search coded in Visual Basic Console

```vb
Module Module1
    Sub main()
        Dim dictionary = New Dictionary(Of String, String) From {
            {"England", "London"},
            {"France", "Paris"},
            {"Germany", "Berlin"}}
        Dim key As String
        Console.Write("Enter the key: ")
        key = Console.ReadLine
        If dictionary.ContainsKey(key) Then
            Console.WriteLine(dictionary(key))
        Else
            Console.WriteLine("Not found")
        End If
        Console.ReadLine()
    End Sub
End Module
```

It is worth noting that unlike an array or list, there is no known order to the items in a dictionary due to the hashing function. Even though England was entered first into the dictionary in the code, it is not necessarily the first item in the structure. Therefore, it doesn't make sense to try to return an item from an index. Some languages support such commands, but the returned value often seems like a random item.

Efficiency of the dictionary

Time complexity			Space complexity
Best case	Average case	Worst case	
O(1) Constant	O(1) Constant	O(n) Linear	O(n) Linear

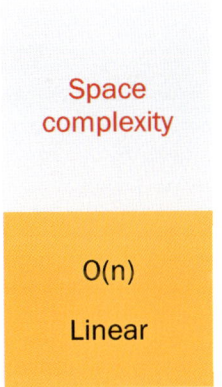

The dictionary data type aims to be extremely efficient, returning a value without having to search for the key in the data set. The implementation of the dictionary data type is abstracted from the programmer. That means we cannot know exactly how the programming language is facilitating the actual storage and retrieval of items from the dictionary. Therefore, it is not possible to accurately determine the efficiency. However, the aim with all key-value pair approaches is to achieve an average constant time complexity — O(1) — for searching, adding and deleting data from a dictionary.

In the worst case, either due to rehashing being necessary as items are added or the implementation of the data type itself, a dictionary could be of linear complexity — O(n) — although this is unlikely in most cases.

Did you know?

Dictionary data structures can also be implemented using a self-balancing binary tree. The advantage of this is that the time complexity can be reduced to O(log n) in the worst case. It is important that the binary tree is balanced to achieve this efficiency. Therefore, the structure of the tree is updated regularly using rotations. It could be argued that this additional overhead makes the implementation less efficient.

Essential algorithms for A level Computer Science

List

| OCR AS Level | OCR A Level | AQA AS Level | AQA A Level |
| WJEC AS Level | WJEC A Level | BTEC Nationals | BTEC Highers |

A list is a collection of elements of different data types. In practice, a list is either an array in disguise or an implementation of a linked list (see higher order data structures). An array is typically used if the limits of the structure are known when the program is written — for example, we know chess is played on an 8x8 board. Conversely, a list is used when the number of items is more variable such as a player's inventory in an RPG game. In reality, either an array or a list can usually be used for the same purpose. Some programming languages support both arrays and lists while some only support one or the other.

A list declaration and assignment in Python:

```
items = ["Florida","Georgia","Delaware","Alabama","California"]
```

A list declaration and assignment in Visual Basic Console:

```
Dim items = New List(Of String) From {"Florida", "California", "Delaware", "Alabama", "Georgia"}
```

Although a list should support elements of different data types, some programming languages require items in a list to be of the same data type, largely because the list is implemented as an array with methods to add and delete data from the structure. Two-dimensional arrays can also be implemented as a list of lists:

List of lists declared In Visual Basic Console:

```
Dim items As New List(Of List(Of String))
```

Unlike arrays, a list is considered to be a **dynamic data structure** because the data it holds increases and decreases the size of the structure at run-time. As a result, lists are usually considered more memory-efficient than arrays, although this does depend entirely on the purpose and use of the structure.

Unlike arrays, which use an index with contiguous memory space, lists can occupy any free memory space and do not need to be stored contiguously. Instead, each item in the list points to the memory location of the next item in the structure. A truly dynamic list takes memory from the heap (a place in memory where data structures are stored) as items are added to the list and returns memory to the heap when items are deleted.

However, in some programming languages, lists are actually arrays in disguise, so it is possible to use an index to refer to a particular element too. Equally, a searching algorithm such as a linear search can also be used to retrieve a specific element from an index. On a true list, this operation will be less efficient than using an index to specify a relative address for an element of an array.

Applications of a list

Lists are used in situations where a set of related data items need to be stored, especially when the number of items is variable and not known in advance. Some programming languages may not support lists — instead, a programmer would need to create their own linked list structure.

Operations on a list

Typical operations that can be performed on a list include:

- Add: append or insert an item in the list
- Delete: remove an item from the list
- Next: moves to the next item in the list
- Previous: moves to the previous item in a list
- Traverse: a linear search through the list

Due to the fact that lists are sometimes implemented with arrays, some programming languages facilitate the use of indexes with lists. Therefore, it might be possible to retrieve or assign a specific item in a list by using the index.

Craig'n'Dave videos

https://craigndave.org/algorithm-list

A list illustrated

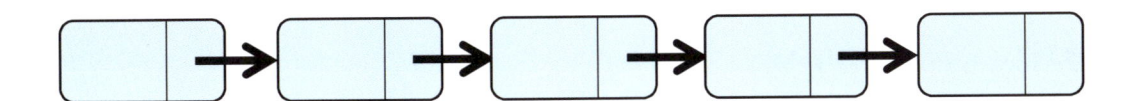

Did you know?

Immutable means the size and data in a structure cannot change at run-time.

Mutable means the size and data in a structure can change at run-time.

Lists are mutable. A **tuple** is an immutable list.

Essential algorithms for A level Computer Science

Efficiency of a list

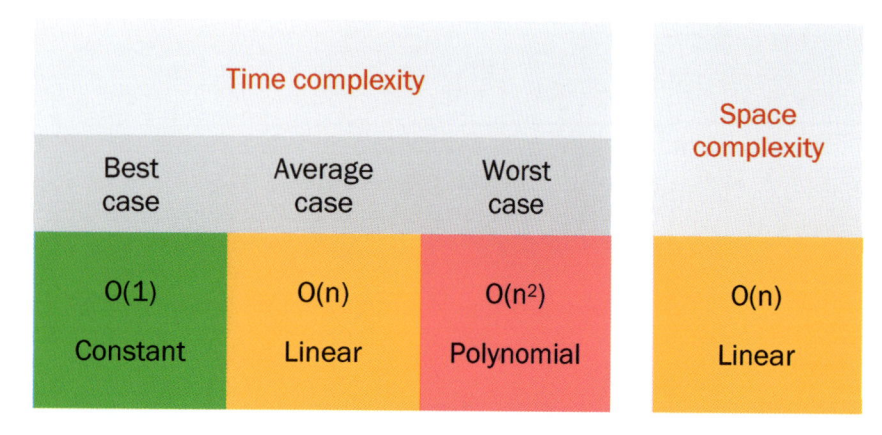

Time complexity			Space complexity
Best case	Average case	Worst case	
O(1) Constant	O(n) Linear	O(n^2) Polynomial	O(n) Linear

Since a list is considered a dynamic data structure, its memory footprint is not known in advance, so it has a linear space complexity: O(n).

Calculating the time complexity with a list depends on the algorithms being implemented with it. Adding an item to the start of a list can be done immediately, so at best, it has a constant time complexity: O(1). Adding an item into the list or removing an item requires the item to be found. Therefore, a linear search would be required, resulting in linear complexity: O(n).

With lists of lists, if a nested loop is required to iterate over all the elements, it becomes polynomial: O(n2). However, this is an uncommon use of a list, so its worst-case time complexity is usually stated as linear: O(n).

Did you know?

Although it is widely stated that Python does not support arrays, this is not strictly true. Internally, a list in Python is actually represented as an array. This explains why it is possible to use indexes to reference items in a list in Python.

In summary

Array	Dictionary	List
Elements are all of the same data type	Stores key-value pairs	Elements can be different data types in some languages
Elements are stored in contiguous memory space, making use of an index register	Values are stored in a location determined by a hashing function	Elements are stored in any free memory space, making use of pointers to link elements together
Static data structure	Dynamic data structure	Dynamic data structure
Uses an index to retrieve an element at a specific location	Uses a hash table search to retrieve a value from a key	Uses a linear search to retrieve an element at a specific location
Indexes are not deleted, so when data items are removed from an array, the element is set to an empty string or null	Key-value pairs can be deleted	Elements can be deleted

HIGHER ORDER DATA STRUCTURES

Supported by some programming languages within the command set, programmers often implement these structures using the fundamental data structures as building blocks.

Binary Tree

A binary tree is a data structure consisting of nodes and pointers. It is a special case of a graph where each node can only have zero, one or two pointers. Each pointer connects to a different node.

The first node is known as the root node. The connected nodes are known as child nodes, while the nodes at the very bottom of the structure are referred to as leaf nodes.

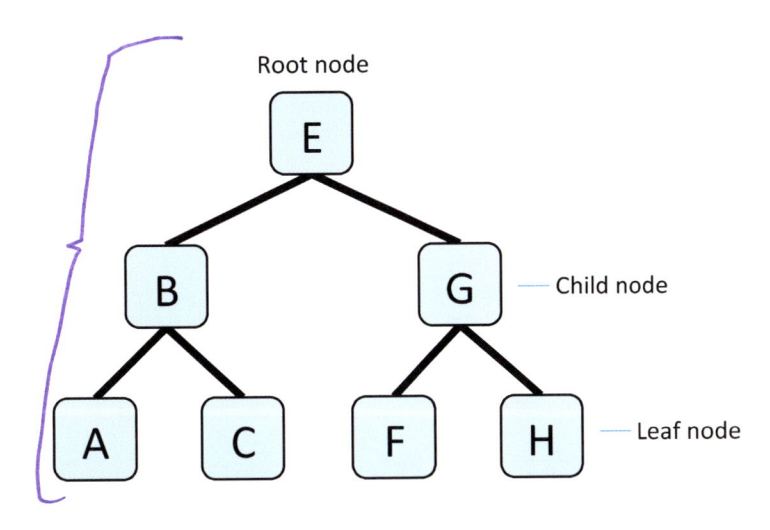

```
                    Root node
                       │
                       E
                      / \
                     /   \
                    B     G  ── Child node
                   / \   / \
                  A   C F   H  ── Leaf node
```

Since a binary tree is essentially a graph, the nodes and pointers can also be described as vertices and edges, respectively. Binary trees can be represented in memory with dictionaries:

```
tree = {"E":["B","G"],"B":["A","C"],"G":["F","H"],"A":[],"C":[],"F":[],"H":[]}
```
→ arrays

See the "Graphs" chapter for an alternative implementation with associated breadth and depth-first algorithms that can also be applied to binary trees.

It is more common to see a binary tree represented as objects consisting of a node with a left and right pointer. Typically, when implementing the binary tree, a node has its left and/or right pointer set to be nothing or null if there is no child node.

Applications of a binary tree

Binary trees have many uses in computer science. These include database applications where efficient searching and sorting is necessary without moving items, which is slow to execute. They can also be found in wireless networking, router tables and scheduling processes in operating systems. Implementations of the A* pathfinding algorithm can use trees. Huffman coding used for compression algorithms such as jpeg and mp3 makes use of binary trees, as does cryptography (GGM trees). Binary trees are also useful for performing arithmetic using reverse Polish notation, which negates the need to use brackets to define the order of precedence for operators in an expression.

↓ An algorithm to solves the shortest route between 2 pointers

Essential algorithms for A level Computer Science

Operations on a binary tree

Typical operations that can be performed on a binary tree include:

- Add: adds a new node to the tree
- Delete: removes a node from the tree
- Binary search: returns the data stored in a node
- Pre-order traversal: a type of depth-first search
- In-order traversal: a type of depth-first search
- Post-order traversal: a type of depth-first search
- Breadth-first search: traverses the tree, starting at the root node, visiting each node at the same level before going deeper into the structure

A traversal refers to the process of visiting each node in a binary tree only once. It is also a term commonly used with graphs. A traversal is required to find, update and output the data in a node.

Craig'n'Dave videos

https://www.craigndave.org/algorithm-binary-tree

Adding an item to a binary tree in simple-structured English

1. Check there is free memory for a new node. Output an error if not.
2. Create a new node and insert data into it.
3. If the binary tree is empty:
    a. The new node becomes the first item. Create a start pointer to it.
4. If the binary tree is not empty:
    a. Start at the root node.
    b. If the new node should be placed before the current node, follow the left pointer.
    c. If the new node should be placed after the current node, follow the right pointer.
    d. Repeat from step 4b until the leaf node is reached.
    e. If the new node should be placed before the current node, set the left pointer to be the new node.
    f. If the new node should be placed before the current node, set the right pointer to be the new node.

16

Higher order data structures

Adding an item to a binary tree illustrated (To add D)

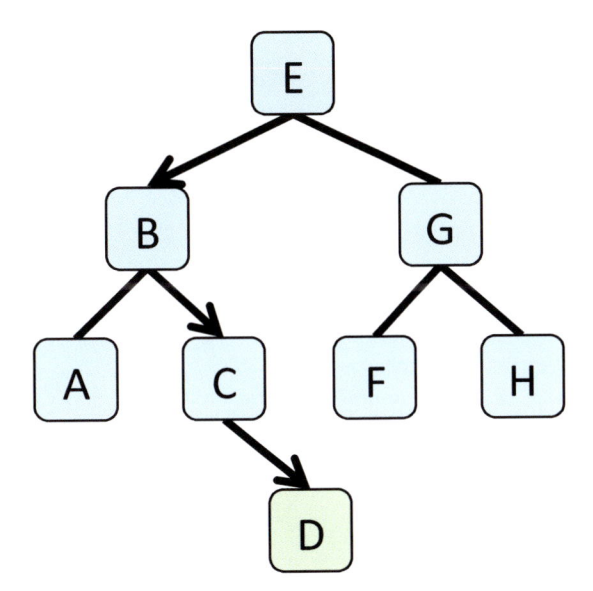

```
            E
           / \
          B   G
         / \ / \
        A  C F  H
            \
             D
```

Start at the root node. D is [less than] E; follow the left pointer. D is more than B; follow the right pointer. D is more than C; create a right pointer from C to D.

alphabetically

💡 Did you know?

The maximum efficiency of a binary tree is achieved when the tree is balanced. That means one branch is not significantly larger than another. A special case of a binary tree, called a self-balancing binary tree, automatically keeps its height small when items are added and deleted by moving nodes within the structure to maintain the balance.

A self-balancing operation decreases the efficiency of adding and deleteing items but increases the efficiency of searching the structure. In this case, it is a very efficient way to implement a dictionary.

Essential algorithms for A level Computer Science

Pseudocode for adding an item to a binary tree

```
If not memoryfull Then
        new_node = New Node
        new_node.left_pointer = Null
        new_node.right_pointer = Null
        current_node = start_pointer
        If current_node == Null Then
                start_pointer = new_node
        Else
                While current_node != Null
                        previous_node = current_node
                        If new_node < current_node Then
                                current_node = current_node.left_pointer
                        Else
                                current_node = current_node.right_pointer
                        End If
                End While
                If current_node < previous_node Then
                        previous_node.left_pointer = new_node
                Else
                        previous_node.rigth_pointer = new_node
                End If
        End If
End If
```

Did you know?

Like all data structures, a binary tree can be represented using an array. A binary tree requires a two dimensional array.

The root node E is stored at the first index because items are entered into the array as they are added. A feature of a binary tree is that items can be traversed in order, even though they were not entered in order. A binary tree negates the need for a sorting algorithm.

Node E is connected to B (index 1) and G (index 3).

0	E	1	3
1	B	2	4
2	A		
3	G	5	6
4	C		7
5	F		
6	H		
7	D		

Deleting an item from a binary tree in simple-structured English

Firstly, we need to find the node to delete in the structure.

1. Start at the root node.
2. While the current node exists and it is not the one to be deleted:
    a. Set the previous node to be the current node.
    b. If the item to be deleted is less than the current node, follow the left pointer.
    c. If the item to be deleted is greater than the current node, follow the right pointer.

Assuming the node exists and therefore has been found, there are three possibilities that need to be considered when deleting a node from a binary tree:

   i. The node is a leaf node and has no children.
   ii. The node has one child.
   iii. The node has two children.

The node has no children

3. If the previous node is greater than the current node, the previous node's left pointer is set to null.
4. If the previous node is less than the current node, the previous node's right pointer is set to null.

The node has one child

5. If the current node is on the left of the previous node:
    a. Set the previous node's left pointer to the current node's left child.
6. If the current node is on the right of the previous node:
    a. Set the previous node's right pointer to the current node's right child.

Essential algorithms for A level Computer Science

The node has two children

In this situation, we can make use of the fact that the data in a binary tree can be represented in a different way. For example:

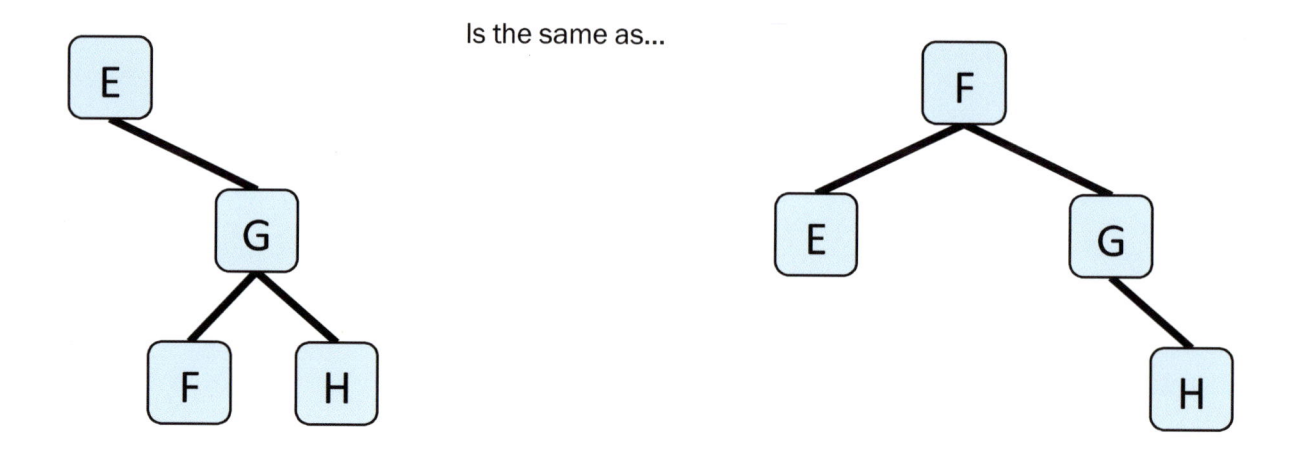

Is the same as...

One approach to deleting node G is to find the smallest value in the right sub-tree (known as the successor) and move it to the position occupied by G. The smallest value in the right sub-tree will always be the left-most node in the right-sub tree. The approach is known as the Hibbard deletion algorithm. In the example above, there is a special case because there is no left sub-tree from node H. Therefore, we can move H into the position occupied by G.

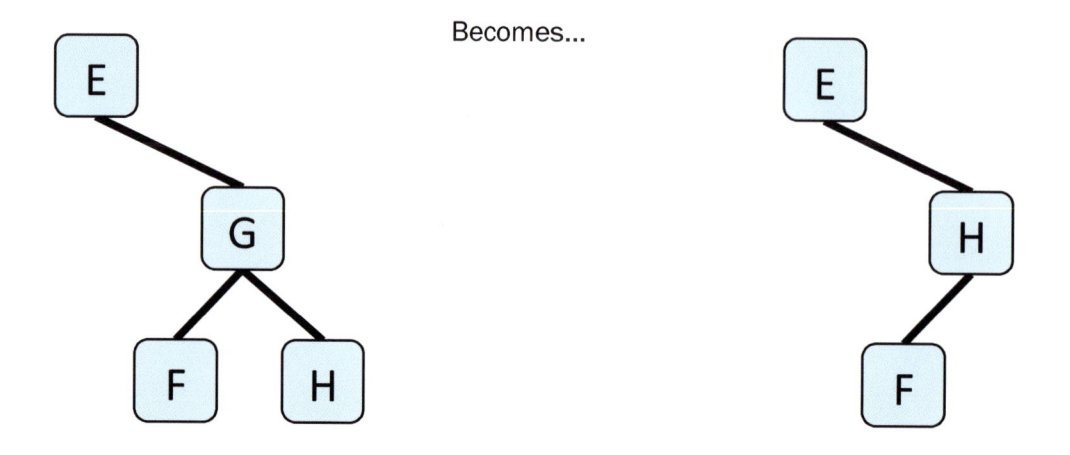

Becomes...

Notice the tree has become unbalanced, as F could now be the root node with E to the left and H to the right. Therefore, there is an impact on the efficiency of algorithms on binary trees when nodes are added and deleted over time.

As with all algorithms, there are alternative approaches, depending on how the structure is implemented by the programmer. One alternative could be to use the predecessor node (the right-most node in the left sub-tree) instead of the successor node. A simple alternative would be to introduce another attribute to each node to flag whether the node is deleted or not and skip deleted nodes when traversing the tree. However, this approach does increase the space complexity as nodes are added and deleted.

Higher order data structures

Hibbard deletion

7. If a right node exists, find the smallest leaf node in the right sub-tree.
    a. Change the current node to the smallest leaf node.
    b. Remove the smallest leaf node.
8. If there is no left sub-tree from the right node then:
    a. Set the current node to be the current node's right pointer.
    b. Set the current node's right pointer to be null.

Deleting an item to a binary tree illustrated

Node has no children:

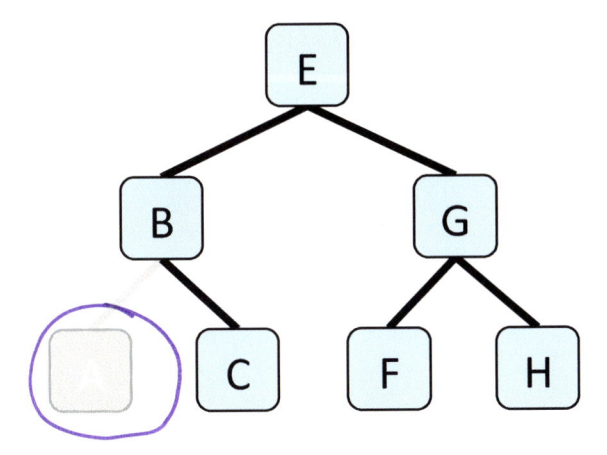

The node can simply be removed. The previous node's left or right pointer is set to null.

Node has one child:

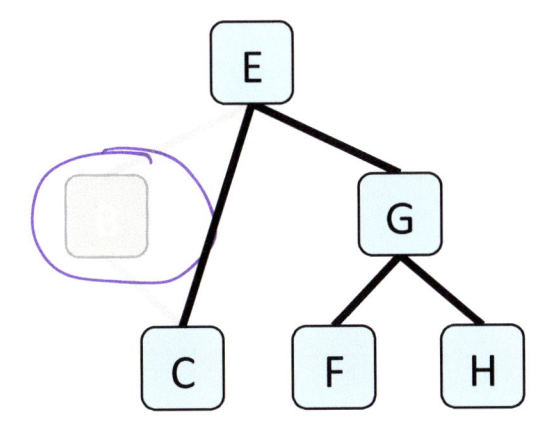

Here, B is being deleted. The previous node's left or right pointer is set to the left or right pointer of the node being deleted. In this case, E's left pointer becomes C.

Essential algorithms for A level Computer Science

G is to be deleted. It has two children:

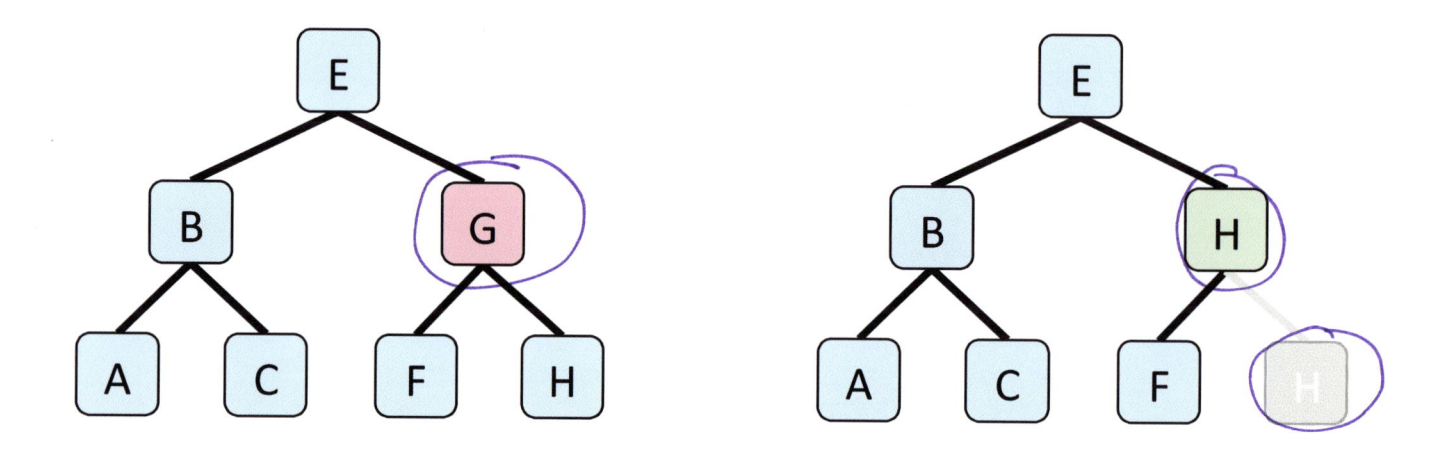

In this special case, there is no left sub-tree from H, so G is replaced with H and its right pointer is set to null. An example with a left sub-tree is shown below.

F is to be deleted. It has two children:

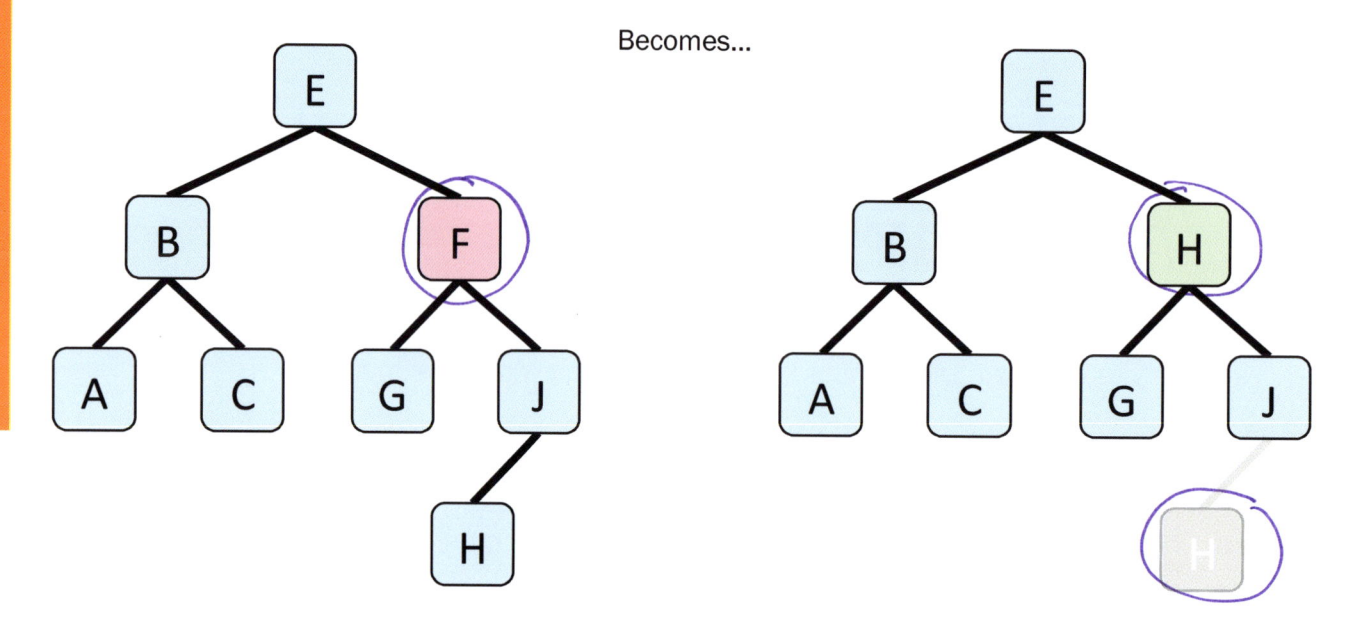

Becomes...

Here F is illustrated as being deleted. The lowest node in the right sub-tree is H. F is replaced with H, and J's left pointer is set to null. However, it is a mistake to assume that it's always the first left node from the right sub-tree that is found. That is not the case. It is the left-most leaf node that is swapped. Therefore, if H had a left pointer, that would be followed until the leaf node is found.

Pseudocode for deleting an item from a binary tree

```
current_node = root node                    ?
while current_node != null and current_node != item
        previous_node = current_node
        if item < current_node.data Then
                current_node = current_node.left_pointer
        Else
                current_node = current_node.right_pointer
        End If
If current_node != null then
        If current_node.left_pointer == null and current_node.right_pointer == null Then
                If previous_node.data > current_node.data Then
                        previous_node.left_pointer = null
                Else
                        previous_node.right_pointer = null
                End If
        Elseif current_node.right_pointer == null Then
                If previous_node.data > current_node.data Then
                        previous_node.left_pointer = current_node.left_pointer
                Else
                        previous_node.right_pointer = current_node.left_pointer
                End If
                If previous_node.data < current_node.data Then
                        previous_node.left_pointer = current_node.right_pointer
                Else
                        previous_node.right_pointer = current_node.right_pointer
                End If
        Else
                right_node = current_node.right_pointer
                If right_node.left_pointer != null Then
                        smallest_node = right_node
                        While smallest_node.left_pointer != null
                                previous_node = smallest_node
                                smallest_node = smallest_node.right_pointer
                        End While
                        current_node.data = smallest_node.data
                        previous_node.left_pointer = null
                End If
        End If
End If
```

Pseudocode for deleting an item from a binary tree

Essential algorithms for A level Computer Science

Pre-order traversal (depth-first search) in simple-structured English

Pre-order traversal — a variation of a depth-first search — is used to create a copy of a binary tree or return prefix expressions in Polish notation, which can be used by programming language interpreters to evaluate syntax. It is worth remembering that traversals can also be performed on graphs.

The algorithm can be described as "Node-Left-Right":

1. Start at the root node.
2. Output the node.
3. Follow the left pointer and repeat from step 2 recursively until there is no pointer to follow.
4. Follow the right pointer and repeat from step 2 recursively until there is no pointer to follow.

Pre-order traversal illustrated

If illustrations help you remember, this is how you can picture a pre-order traversal on a binary tree:

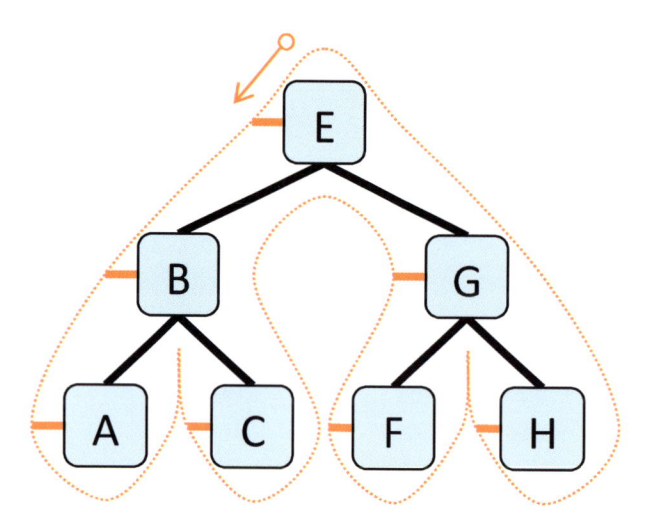

Note the markers on the left side of each node. As you traverse the tree, starting from the root, the nodes are only output when you pass the marker: E, B, A, C, G, F, H. You can illustrate like this in exams to demonstrate your understanding of the algorithm.

HIGHER ORDER DATA STRUCTURES

24

Higher order data structures

Pseudocode for a pre-order traversal

```
Procedure preorder(current_node)
    If current_node != null Then
        Print(current_node.data)
        If current_node.left_pointer != null Then
            preorder(current_node.left_pointer)
        End If
        If current_node.right_pointer != null Then
            preorder(current_node.right_pointer)
        End If
    End If
End procedure
```

In-order traversal (depth-first search) in simple-structured English

In-order traversal — a variation of a depth-first search — is used to output the contents of the binary tree in order. One of the significant advantages of the binary tree is that it automatically sorts the contents of the structure without moving data, irrespective of the order in which the data arrived. This negates the need for an insertion sort, for example. It is worth remembering that traversals can also be performed on graphs.

The algorithm can be described as "Left-Node-Right":

1. Start at the root node.
2. Follow the left pointer and repeat from step 2 recursively until there is no pointer to follow.
3. Output the node.
4. Follow the right pointer and repeat from step 2 recursively until there is no pointer to follow.

Did you know?

A common mistake is to forget that all traversals — including pre-order, in-order and post-order — always follow the left path first, unless you want to output the items in reverse order.

Essential algorithms for A level Computer Science

In-order traversal illustrated

If illustrations help you remember, this is how you can picture an in-order traversal on a binary tree:

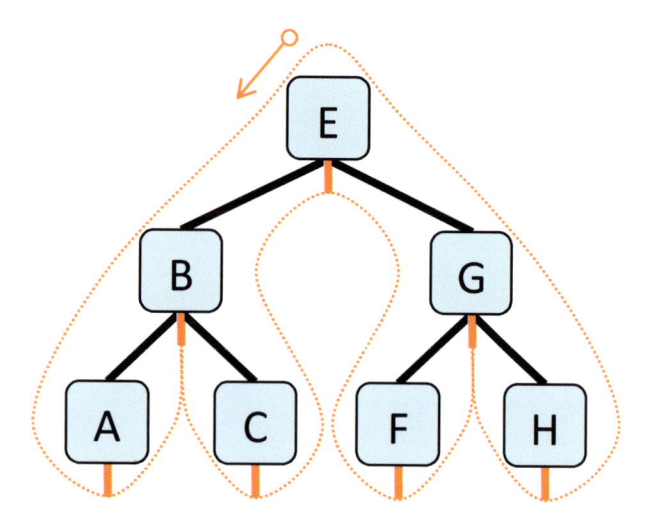

Note the markers on the bottom of each node. As you traverse the tree, starting from the root, the nodes are only output when you pass the marker: A, B, C, E, F, G, H. You can illustrate like this in exams to demonstrate your understanding of the algorithm.

To output the nodes in reverse order, you simply reverse the algorithm by following the right pointers before outputting the node, and then following the left pointers.

Pseudocode for an in-order traversal

```
Procedure preorder(current_node)
    If current_node != null Then
        If current_node.left_pointer != null Then
            preorder(current_node.left_pointer)
        End If
        Print(current_node.data)
        If current_node.right_pointer != null Then
            preorder(current_node.right_pointer)
        End If
    End If
End procedure
```

Post-order traversal (depth-first search) in simple-structured English

A post-order traversal — a variation of a depth-first search — is used to delete a binary tree. It is also useful to output post-fix expressions that can be used to evaluate mathematical expressions without the need for brackets. This is how arithmetic logic units work in stack-machine computers and it was popular in pocket calculators until the early 2010s. It is worth remembering that traversals can also be performed on graphs.

The algorithm can be described as "Left-Right-Node":

1. Start at the root node.
2. Follow the left pointer and repeat from step 2 recursively until there is no pointer to follow.
3. Follow the right pointer and repeat from step 2 recursively until there is no pointer to follow
4. Output the node.

Post-order traversal illustrated

If illustrations help you remember, this is how you can picture a post-order traversal on a binary tree:

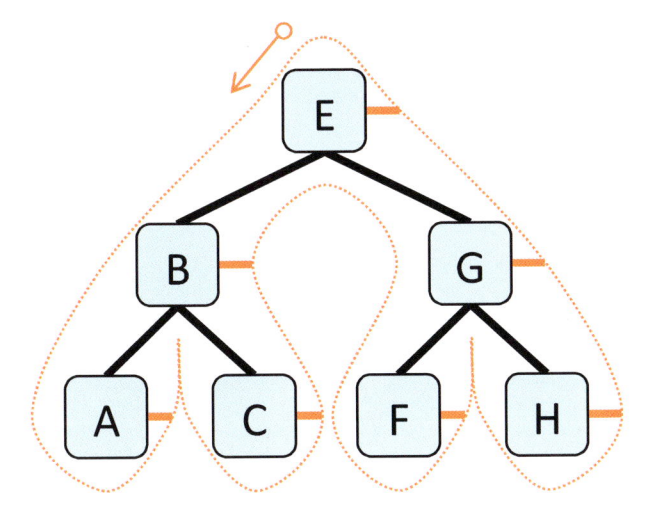

Note the markers on the right side of each node. As you traverse the tree, starting from the root, the nodes are only output when you pass the marker: A, C, B, F, H, G, E. You can illustrate like this in exams to demonstrate your understanding of the algorithm.

Essential algorithms for A level Computer Science

Pseudocode for a post-order traversal

```
Procedure preorder(current_node)
    If current_node != null Then
        If current_node.left_pointer != null Then
            preorder(current_node.left_pointer)
        End If
        If current_node.right_pointer != null Then
            preorder(current_node.right_pointer)
        End If
        Print(current_node.data)
    End If
End procedure
```

Breadth-first search using a binary tree in simple-structured English

Visiting each node on the same level of a tree before going deeper is an example of a breadth-first search. Although commonly associated with graphs, a binary tree can also be traversed in this way, but its implementation does require a queue structure.

1. Start at the root node.

2. While the current node exists:

    a. Output the current node.

    b. If the current node has a left child, enqueue the left node.

    c. If the current node has a right child, enqueue the right node.

    d. Dequeue and set the current node to the dequeued node.

Breadth-first search on a binary tree illustrated

If illustrations help you remember, this is how you can picture a post-order traversal on a binary tree:

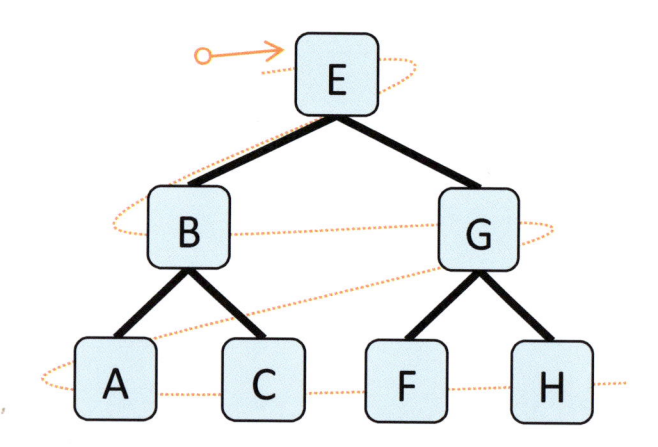

Pseudocode for a breadth-first search on a binary tree

```
current_node = root_node
While current_node != null
    Print(current_node)
    If current_node.left_pointer Then enqueue(current_node.left_pointer)
    If current_node.right_pointer Then enqueue(current_node.right_pointer)
    current_node = dequeue()
```

Binary tree coded in Python

```python
class binary_tree:

    class node:
        data = None
        left_pointer = None
        right_pointer = None

    start = None

    def add(self,item):
        #Check memory overflow
        try:
            new_node = binary_tree.node()
            new_node.data = item
            current_node = self.start
            new_node.left_pointer = None
            new_node.right_pointer = None
            #Tree is empty
            if current_node == None:
                self.start = new_node
            else:
                #Find correct position in the tree
                while current_node != None:
                    previous = current_node
                    if item < current_node.data:
                        current_node = current_node.left_pointer
                    else:
                        current_node = current_node.right_pointer
                if item < previous.data:
                    previous.left_pointer = new_node
                else:
                    previous.right_pointer = new_node
            return True
        except:
            return False

    def delete(self,item):
        #Using Hibbard's algorithm (leftmost node of right sub-tree is the successor)
```

```python
        #Find the node to delete
        current_node = self.start
        while current_node != None and current_node.data != item:
            previous = current_node
            if item < current_node.data:
                current_node = current_node.left_pointer
            else:
                current_node = current_node.right_pointer

        #Handle 3 cases depending on the number of child nodes
        if current_node != None:
            if current_node.left_pointer == None and current_node.right_pointer == None:
                #Node has no children
                if previous.data > current_node.data:
                    previous.left_pointer = None
                else:
                    previous.right_pointer = None
            elif current_node.right_pointer == None:
                #Node has one left child
                if previous.data > current_node.data:
                    previous.left_pointer = current_node.left_pointer
                else:
                    previous.right_pointer = current_node.left_pointer
            elif current_node.left_pointer == None:
                #Node has one right child
                if previous.data < current_node.data:
                    previous.left_pointer = current_node.right_pointer
                else:
                    previous.right_pointer = current_node.right_pointer
            else:
                #Node has two children
                right_node = current_node.right_pointer
                if right_node.left_pointer != None:
                    #Find the smallest value in the right sub-tree (successor node)
                    smallest = right_node
                    while smallest.left_pointer != None:
                        previous = smallest
                        smallest = smallest.left_pointer
                    #Change the deleted node value to the smallest value
                    current_node.data = smallest.data
                    #Remove the successor node
                    previous.left_pointer = None
                else:
                    #Handle special case of no left sub-tree from right node
                    current_node.data = right_node.data
                    current_node.right_pointer = None


    def preorder(self,current_node):
        if current_node != None:
```

```python
            #Visit each node: NLR
            print(current_node.data)
            if current_node.left_pointer != None:
                self.preorder(current_node.left_pointer)
            if current_node.right_pointer != None:
                self.preorder(current_node.right_pointer)

    def inorder(self,current_node):
        if current_node != None:
            #Visit each node: LNR
            if current_node.left_pointer != None:
                self.inorder(current_node.left_pointer)
            print(current_node.data)
            if current_node.right_pointer != None:
                self.inorder(current_node.right_pointer)

    def postorder(self,current_node):
        if current_node != None:
            #Visit each node: LRN
            if current_node.left_pointer != None:
                self.postorder(current_node.left_pointer)
            if current_node.right_pointer != None:
                self.postorder(current_node.right_pointer)
            print(current_node.data)
```

Adding items to a binary tree object in Python

```python
items = ["E","B","G","A","C","F","H"]
bt = binary_tree()
for index in range(0,len(items)):
    bt.add(items[index])
```

Deleting items from a binary tree object in Python

```python
bt.delete("G")
```

Outputting items from a binary tree object in Python

```python
bt.preorder(bt.start)

bt.inorder(bt.start)
bt.postorder(bt.start)
```

Binary tree coded in Visual Basic Console

```vb
Module Module1
    Public Class binarytree

        Public Class node
            Public data As String
            Public left_pointer As node
            Public right_pointer As node
        End Class

        Public start As node

        Function add(item As String)
            'Check memory overflow
            Try
                Dim new_node As New node
                new_node.data = item
                Dim current_node As node = start
                new_node.left_pointer = Nothing
                new_node.right_pointer = Nothing
                'Tree is empty
                If IsNothing(current_node) Then
                    start = new_node
                Else
                    'Find correct position in the tree
                    Dim previous As node
                    While Not IsNothing(current_node)
                        previous = current_node
                        If item < current_node.data Then
                            current_node = current_node.left_pointer
                        Else
                            current_node = current_node.right_pointer
                        End If
                    End While
                    If item < previous.data Then
                        previous.left_pointer = new_node
                    Else
                        previous.right_pointer = new_node
                    End If
                    Return True
                End If
            Catch
                Return False
            End Try
        End Function

        Sub delete(item As String)
            'Using Hibbard's algorithm (leftmost node of right sub-tree is the successor)
```

```vbnet
            'Find the node
            Dim current_node As node = start
            Dim previous As node
            While Not IsNothing(current_node) And current_node.data <> item
                previous = current_node
                If item < current_node.data Then
                    current_node = current_node.left_pointer
                Else
                    current_node = current_node.right_pointer
                End If
            End While

            'Handle 3 cases depending on the number of child nodes
            If Not IsNothing(current_node) Then
                If IsNothing(current_node.left_pointer) And IsNothing(current_node.right_pointer) Then
                    'Node has no children
                    If previous.data > current_node.data Then
                        previous.left_pointer = Nothing
                    Else
                        previous.right_pointer = Nothing
                    End If
                ElseIf IsNothing(current_node.right_pointer)
                    'Node has one left child
                    If previous.data > current_node.data Then
                        previous.left_pointer = current_node.left_pointer
                    Else
                        previous.right_pointer = current_node.left_pointer
                    End If
                ElseIf IsNothing(current_node.left_pointer)
                    'Node has one right child
                    If previous.data < current_node.data Then
                        previous.left_pointer = current_node.right_pointer
                    Else
                        previous.right_pointer = current_node.right_pointer
                    End If
                Else
                    'Node has two children
                    Dim right_node As node = current_node.right_pointer
                    If Not IsNothing(right_node.left_pointer) Then
                        'Find the smallest value in the right sub-tree
                        Dim smallest As node = current_node.right_pointer
                        While Not IsNothing(smallest.left_pointer)
                            previous = smallest
                            smallest = smallest.left_pointer
                        End While
                        'Change the deleted node value to the smallest value
                        current_node.data = smallest.data
                        'Remove the successor node
                        previous.left_pointer = Nothing
```

```vbnet
                Else
                    'Handle special case of no left sub-tree from right node
                    current_node.data = right_node.data
                    current_node.right_pointer = Nothing
                End If
            End If
        End If
    End Sub

    Sub preorder(current_node As node)
        If Not IsNothing(current_node) Then
            'Visit each node: NLR
            Console.WriteLine(current_node.data)
            If Not IsNothing(current_node.left_pointer) Then
                preorder(current_node.left_pointer)
            End If
            If Not IsNothing(current_node.right_pointer) Then
                preorder(current_node.right_pointer)
            End If
        End If
    End Sub

    Sub inorder(current_node As node)
        If Not IsNothing(current_node) Then
            'Visit each node: LNR
            If Not IsNothing(current_node.left_pointer) Then
                inorder(current_node.left_pointer)
            End If
            Console.WriteLine(current_node.data)
            If Not IsNothing(current_node.right_pointer) Then
                inorder(current_node.right_pointer)
            End If
        End If
    End Sub

    Sub postorder(current_node As node)
        If Not IsNothing(current_node) Then
            'Visit each node: LRN
            If Not IsNothing(current_node.left_pointer) Then
                postorder(current_node.left_pointer)
            End If
            If Not IsNothing(current_node.right_pointer) Then
                postorder(current_node.right_pointer)
            End If
            Console.WriteLine(current_node.data)
        End If
    End Sub

End Class
```

```vb
    'Main program starts here
    Sub Main()

        bt.delete("Delaware")
        bt.inorder(bt.start)
        Console.ReadLine()
    End Sub
End Module
```

Adding items to a binary tree object in Visual Basic Console

```vb
Dim items() As String = {"E", "B", "G", "A", "C", "F", "H"}
        Dim bt As New binarytree
        For index = 0 To items.Length - 1
            bt.add(items(index))
        Next
```

Deleting items from a binary tree object in Visual Basic Console

```vb
bt.delete("G")
```

Outputting items from a binary tree object in Visual Basic Console

```vb
bt.preorder(bt.start)
bt.inorder(bt.start)
bt.postorder(bt.start)
```

Did you know?

A tree traversal is also known as a tree search. While a linked list can only be traversed forwards or backwards, a tree can be traversed in many different ways.

Efficiency of a binary tree

Space complexity of a binary tree

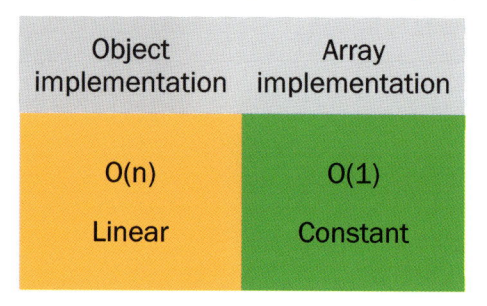

Object implementation	Array implementation
O(n) Linear	O(1) Constant

A binary tree is a dynamic data structure, meaning its memory footprint grows and shrinks as data is added and deleted from the structure when implemented using object-oriented techniques. Using only as much memory as needed is the most efficient way of implementing a binary tree. Alternatively, you could implement a binary tree using a dictionary or an array. With an array, you would be using a static data structure, so the memory footprint would be static, but the size of the structure would also be limited.

Time complexity of operations on a binary tree

Operation	Best case	Average case	Worst case
Storing the binary tree	O(n) Linear	O(n) Linear	O(n) Linear
Add a node	O(log n) Logarithmic	O(log n) Logarithmic	O(n) Linear
Delete a node	O(log n) Logarithmic	O(log n) Logarithmic	O(n) Linear
Binary search	O(1) Constant	O(log n) Logarithmic	O(V) Linear
Traversal	O(V) Linear	O(V) Linear	O(V) Linear

Assuming the binary tree is not pre-populated, to establish the tree from a list of data items will require each item to be added sequentially. However, the input order of the items does not matter — therefore, the number of operations depends on the number of data items: O(n).

Adding, deleting and searching nodes on a binary tree uses a technique called **divide and conquer**. With a balanced tree, the number of items to consider is halved each time a node is visited, providing logarithmic complexity: O(log n). If the tree is unbalanced, it becomes the same as a linear search to determine the location of an item to add or delete, demoting it to linear complexity: O(n).

Balanced tree where each level is complete:

Unbalanced tree holding the same data:

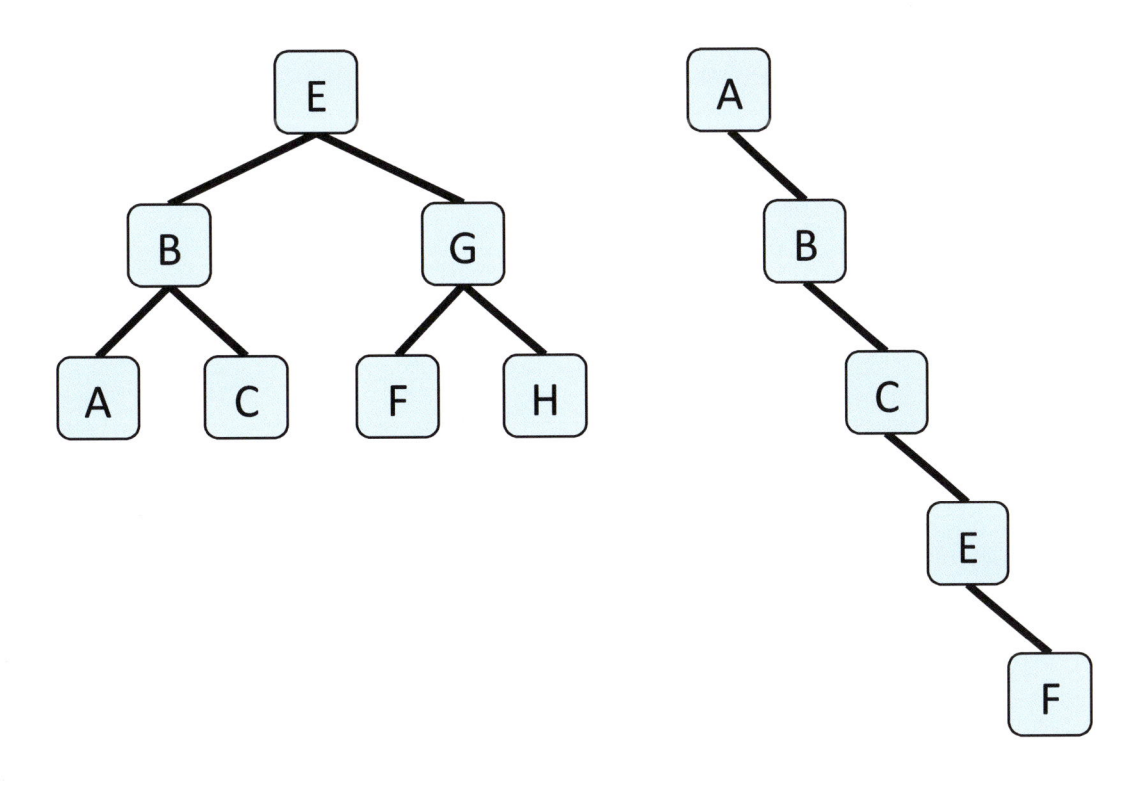

```
            E
           / \
          B   G
         / \ / \
        A  C F  H
```

```
    A
     \
      B
       \
        C
         \
          E
           \
            F
```

In the best-case scenario, the node to be found is the root node, so it can always be found first: O(1).

The traversal algorithms all require each node to be visited. As the number of nodes in the tree increases, so too does the execution time. Therefore, traversals are of linear complexity: O(n).

Essential algorithms for A level Computer Science

Graph

A graph is a data structure consisting of nodes (vertices) and pointers (edges). It differs from a linked list and binary tree because each vertex can have more than one or two edges and point to any vertex in the data structure. The edges can either point in one direction, known as a directed graph, or without specifying a direction (bidirectional), referred to as an undirected graph. Graphs can also be weighted, with each edge given a value representing a relationship such as distance between the vertices. Although it is common to refer to vertices and edges when discussing graphs, this is largely due to their application in mathematics. A vertex can also be referred to as a node and an edge as a pointer.

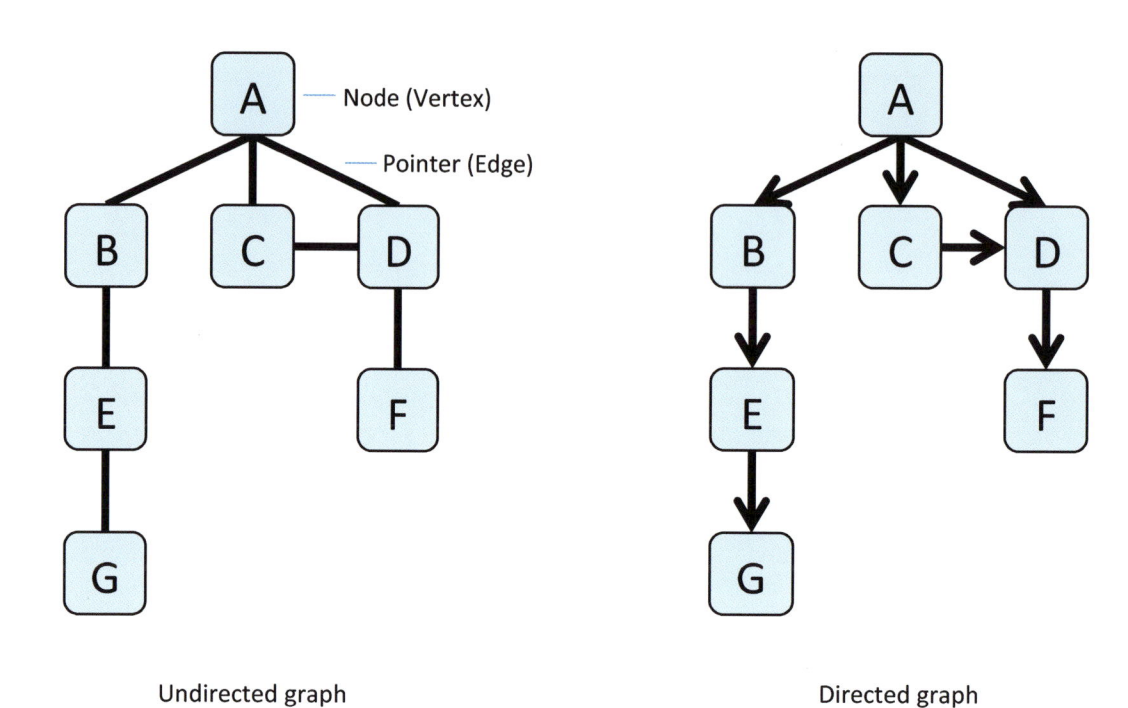

Undirected graph

Directed graph

Typically, the undirected graph illustrated can be represented with the following syntax in Python, although this will differ from language to language:

graph = {"A":["B","C","D"],"B":["A","E"],"C":["A","D"],"D":["A","C","F"],"E":["B","G"],"F":["D"],"G":["E"]}

In pseudocode, this may also be presented as:

Edges { (A,B), (A,C), (A,D), (B,A,), (B,E), (C,A), (C,D), (D,A), (D,C), (D,F), (E,B), (E,G), (F,D), (G,E) }

The directed graph:

graph = {"A":["B","C","D"],"B":["E"],"C":["D"],"D":["F"],"E":["G"],"F":[],"G":[]}

It is also possible for each edge to have an edge value associated with it, typically also referred to as a cost. This is necessary for some algorithms using graph data structures such as Dijkstra's algorithm.

Costs can be defined as:

graph = {"A":["B":2,"C":6,"D":3]

This would mean the edge value between A and B is two, the edge value between A and C is six, and the edge value between A and D is three. Edge values can represent many things between two vertices, including distance, time or bandwidth, depending on what the data structure is being used for.

While it is typical to store graphs as objects or using a dictionary, known as **adjacency lists**, it is also possible to store a graph using an array — or a list of lists. This implementation is known as an **adjacency matrix,** with rows and columns representing vertices and edges respectively.

An example of an adjacency matrix for the undirected graph is shown below. The rows and columns are not usually labelled with the vertices when implementing this method, but they are shown here to aid understanding. A "1" represents an edge existing between the two vertices.

	A	B	C	D	E	F	G
A	0	1	1	1	0	0	0
B	1	0	0	0	1	0	0
C	1	0	0	1	0	0	0
D	1	0	1	0	0	1	0
E	0	1	0	0	0	0	1
F	0	0	0	1	0	0	0
G	0	0	0	0	1	0	0

Typically, this might be declared as:

```
Graph ([[0,1,1,1,0,0,0],
       [1,0,0,0,1,0,0],
       [1,0,0,1,0,0,0],
       [1,0,1,0,0,1,0],
       [0,1,0,0,0,0,1],
       [0,0,0,1,0,0,0],
       [0,0,0,0,1,0,0]])
```

Applications of a graph

Graphs have many uses in computer science — e.g., mapping road networks for navigation systems, storing social network data, resource allocation in operating systems, representing molecular structures and geometry.

Abstraction

It is worth noting that graphs and trees are essentially the same data structure, with a binary tree being a special type of graph. Therefore, operations on a binary tree such as a traversal can also be performed on graph structures too.

In the illustrations below, we see how graph data can remain the same, even though the structure looks different. What is important is not what the graph looks like but which vertices are connected. Using only the necessary detail and discarding unnecessary detail is known as **abstraction**.

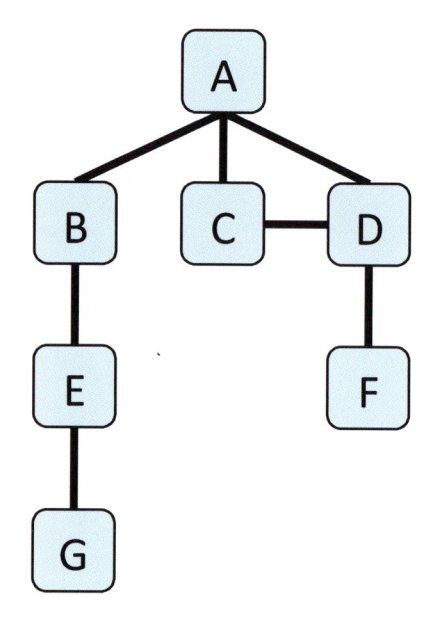

Is the same as:

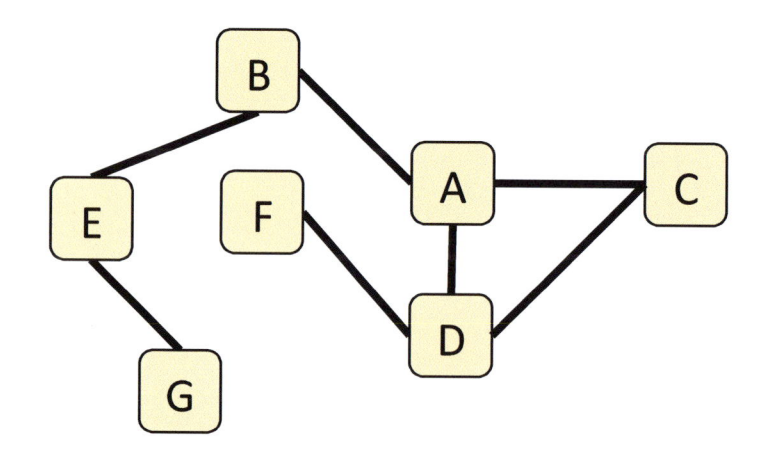

This becomes more apparent when you consider how navigation systems store map data. They simply need to know the type of each road, how long they are and which ones are connected. An obvious example of abstraction is the map of the London Underground. It bears no resemblance to where the stations are located within the city. All that is important is which stations are connected on which line.

Similarly, it is important that students don't concern themselves with how a graph actually looks or what operation is being asked for in an examination. Simply follow the algorithm on the structure given — e.g., a pre-order traversal on a graph, when you might expect that only to be relevant to a binary tree.

Operations on a graph

Typical operations that can be performed on a graph include:

- Adjacent: returns whether there is an edge between two vertices
- Neighbours: returns all the vertices between two vertices
- Add: adds a new vertex to the graph
- Remove: removes a vertex from the graph
- Add edge: adds a new edge to a vertex from another vertex
- Remove edge: removes an edge between two vertices
- Get vertex value: returns the data stored in a vertex
- Set vertex value: sets the data for a vertex
- Get edge value: returns the value of an edge between two vertices
- Set edge value: sets the value of an edge between two vertices
- Depth-first search: traverses the graph, starting at the root vertex, visiting each vertex and exploring each branch as far as possible before backtracking
- Breadth-first search: traverses the graph, starting at the root node, visiting each neighbouring node before moving to the vertices at the next depth
- Pre-order traversal: a type of depth-first search (see binary tree for an example)
- In-order traversal: a type of depth-first search (see binary tree for an example)
- Post-order traversal: a type of depth-first search (see binary tree for an example)

Craig'n'Dave videos

https://www.craigndave.org/algorithm-graph

Essential algorithms for A level Computer Science

Breadth-first search on a graph

The breadth-first search is used to determine the shortest path between vertices on a graph, search engine indexing using a crawler algorithm, finding devices on peer-to-peer networks and broadcasting frames or packets on a network. GPS navigation systems, memory management using Cheney's algorithm and finding nearby people on a social network are all applications of breadth-first searches.

A breadth-first search **requires the use of a queue** data structure.

Breadth-first search in simple-structured English

1. Set the root vertex as the current vertex.
2. If the vertex has an edge that has not been visited:
    a. Enqueue the linked vertex.
    b. Repeat from step 2 until all the edges have been visited.
3. Add the current vertex to the list of visited vertices.
4. Dequeue the queue and set the item removed as the current vertex.
5. Repeat from step 2 until there are no vertices to visit.
6. Output all the visited vertices.

Breadth-first search illustrated

If illustrations help you remember, this is how you can picture a breadth-first search on a graph:

42

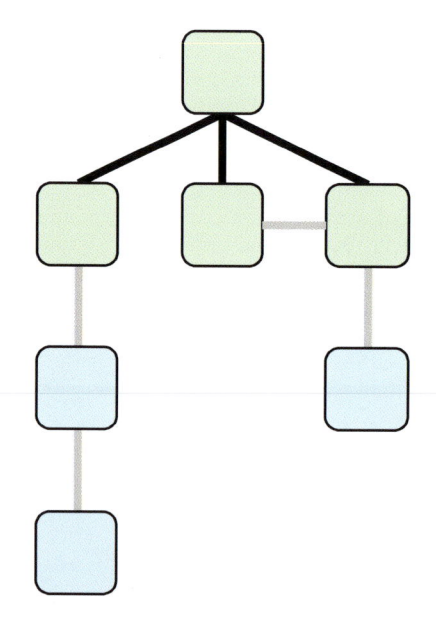

Stepping through the breadth-first search

The front pointer in the queue is represented by the lowercase letter "f." The back pointer in the queue is represented by the lowercase letter "b."

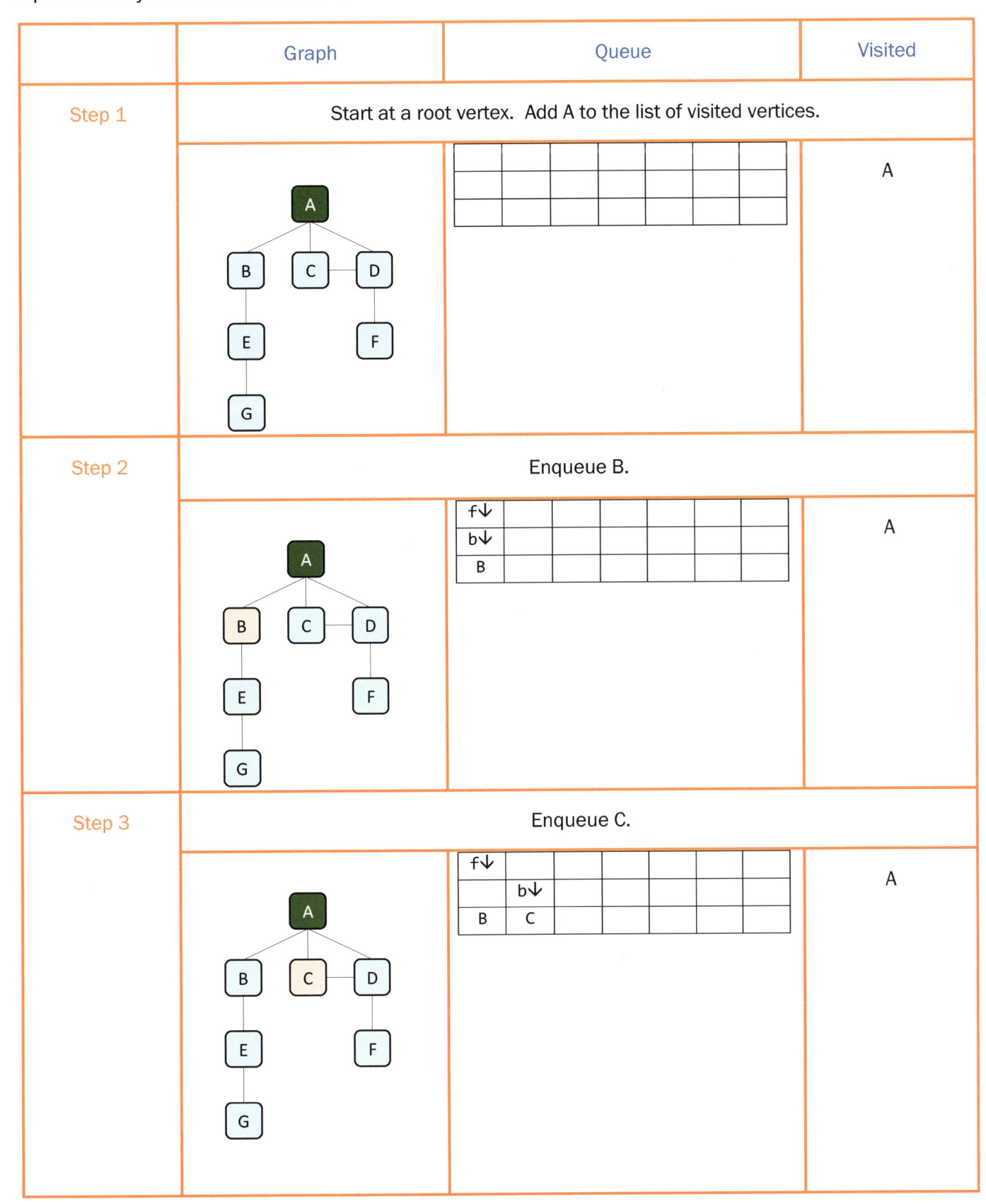

	Graph	Queue	Visited
Step 1	Start at a root vertex. Add A to the list of visited vertices.		
	(Graph with A as root; B, C, D as children of A; E child of B; F child of D; G child of E)	(empty queue)	A
Step 2		Enqueue B.	
	(Same graph, B highlighted)	Queue: f↓ b↓ B	A
Step 3		Enqueue C.	
	(Same graph, C highlighted)	Queue: f↓ B, b↓ C	A

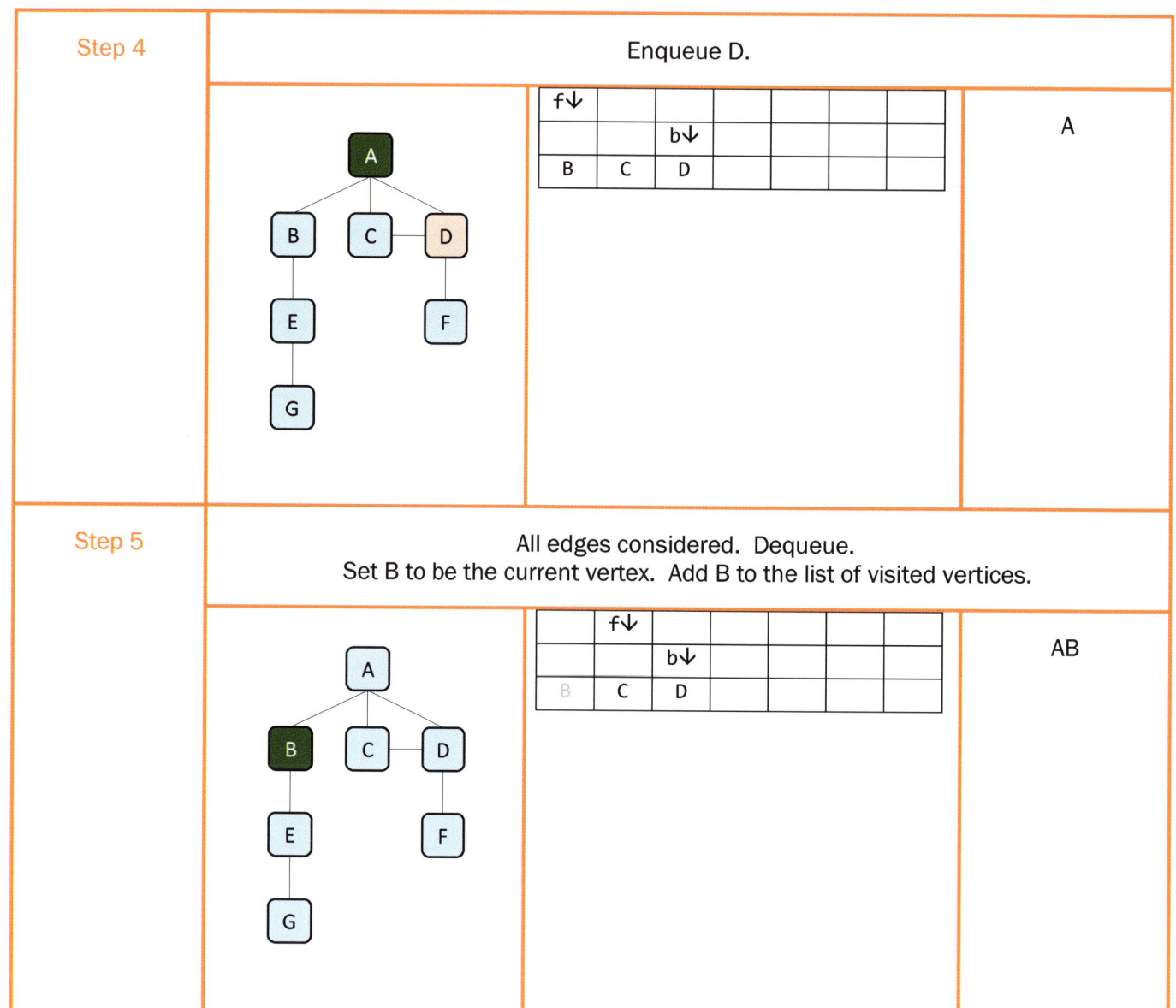

Essential algorithms for A level Computer Science

Step 4	Enqueue D.	
	Tree with A (root), children B, C, D (D highlighted); E child of B; F child of D; G child of E. Queue: f↓ pointing above B; b↓ pointing above D; cells: B, C, D.	A
Step 5	All edges considered. Dequeue. Set B to be the current vertex. Add B to the list of visited vertices.	
	Tree with A (root), children B (highlighted), C, D; E child of B; F child of D; G child of E. Queue: f↓ above C; b↓ above D; cells: B (faded), C, D.	AB

Did you know?

The breadth-first search was invented by Konrad Zuse in 1945. Re-invented in 1959 by Edward Moore, it was used to find the shortest path out of a maze.

Higher order data structures

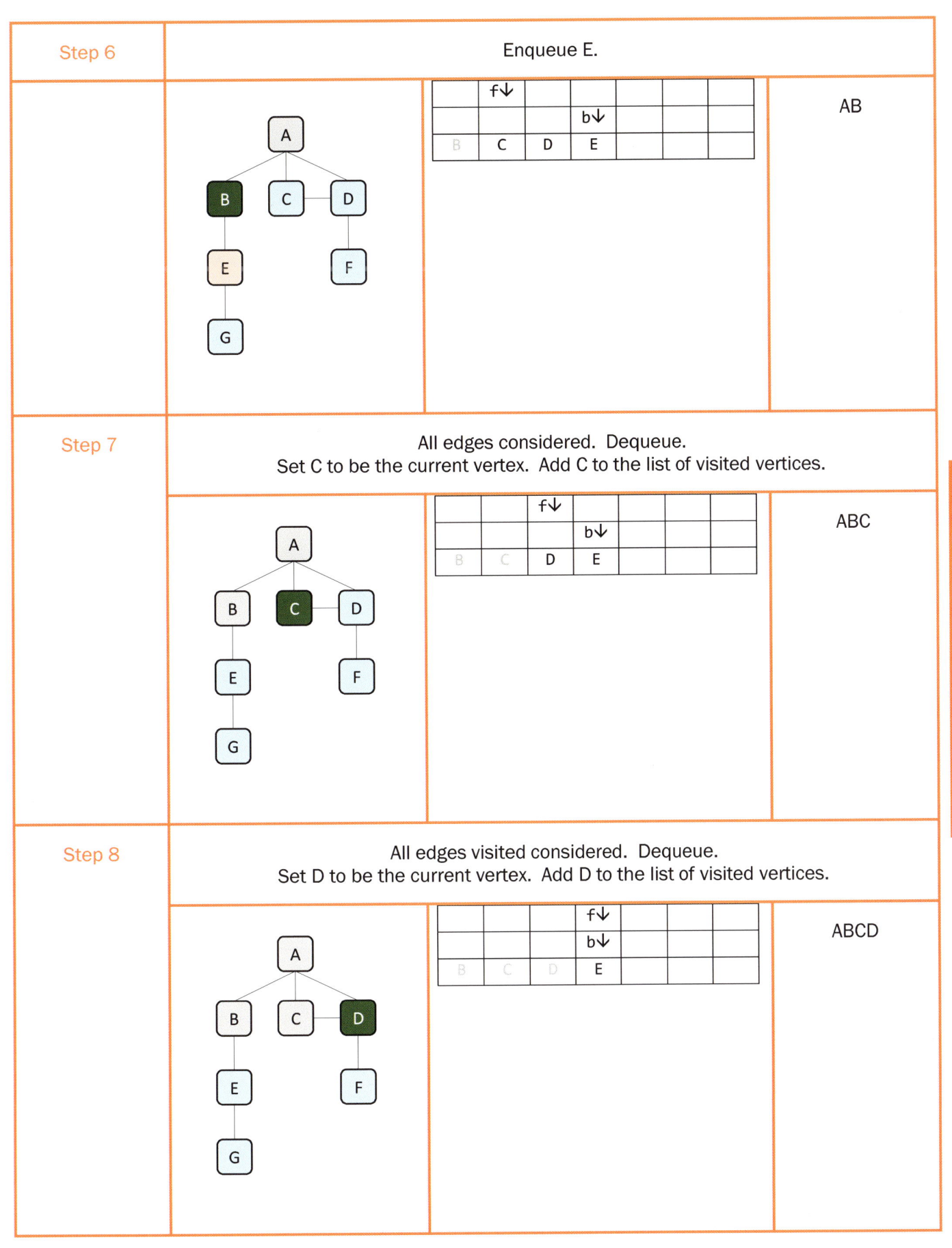

Step 6	Enqueue E.	
	Tree: A-B, A-C, A-D; B-E; D-F; E-G. B is current (dark green), E highlighted. Queue: f↓ over empty; b↓ over E; row: B C D E	AB

Step 7	All edges considered. Dequeue. Set C to be the current vertex. Add C to the list of visited vertices.	
	Tree: A with children B, C, D; E child of B; F child of D; G child of E. C is current (dark green). Queue: f↓ above C; b↓ above E; row: B C D E	ABC

Step 8	All edges visited considered. Dequeue. Set D to be the current vertex. Add D to the list of visited vertices.	
	Tree: same structure. D is current (dark green). Queue: f↓ above D; b↓ above E; row: B C D E	ABCD

45

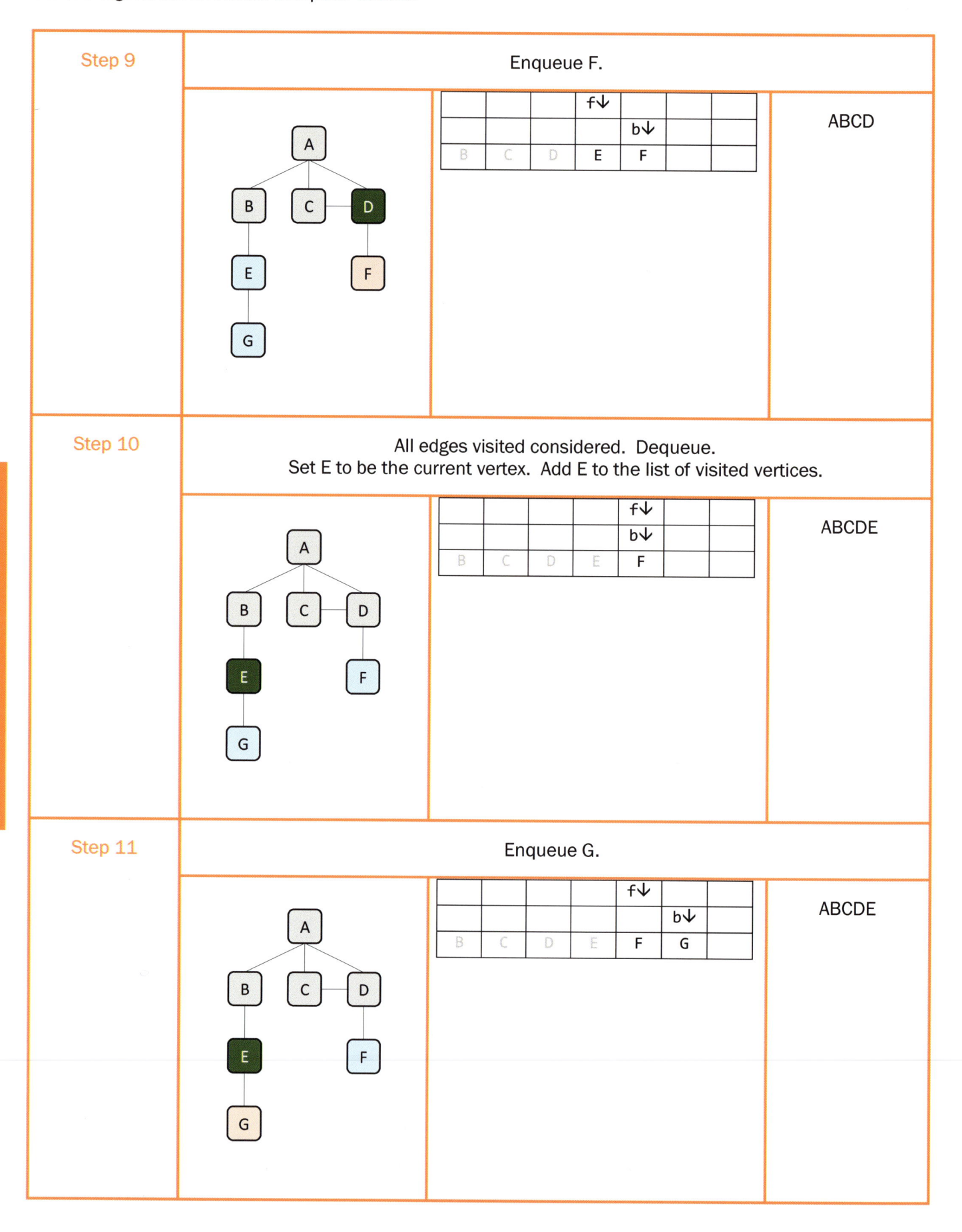

Essential algorithms for A level Computer Science

Step 9	Enqueue F.		ABCD

			f↓		
				b↓	
B	C	D	E	F	

Step 10	All edges visited considered. Dequeue. Set E to be the current vertex. Add E to the list of visited vertices.		ABCDE

			f↓		
			b↓		
B	C	D	E	F	

Step 11	Enqueue G.		ABCDE

			f↓		
				b↓	
B	C	D	E	F	G

46

Higher order data structures

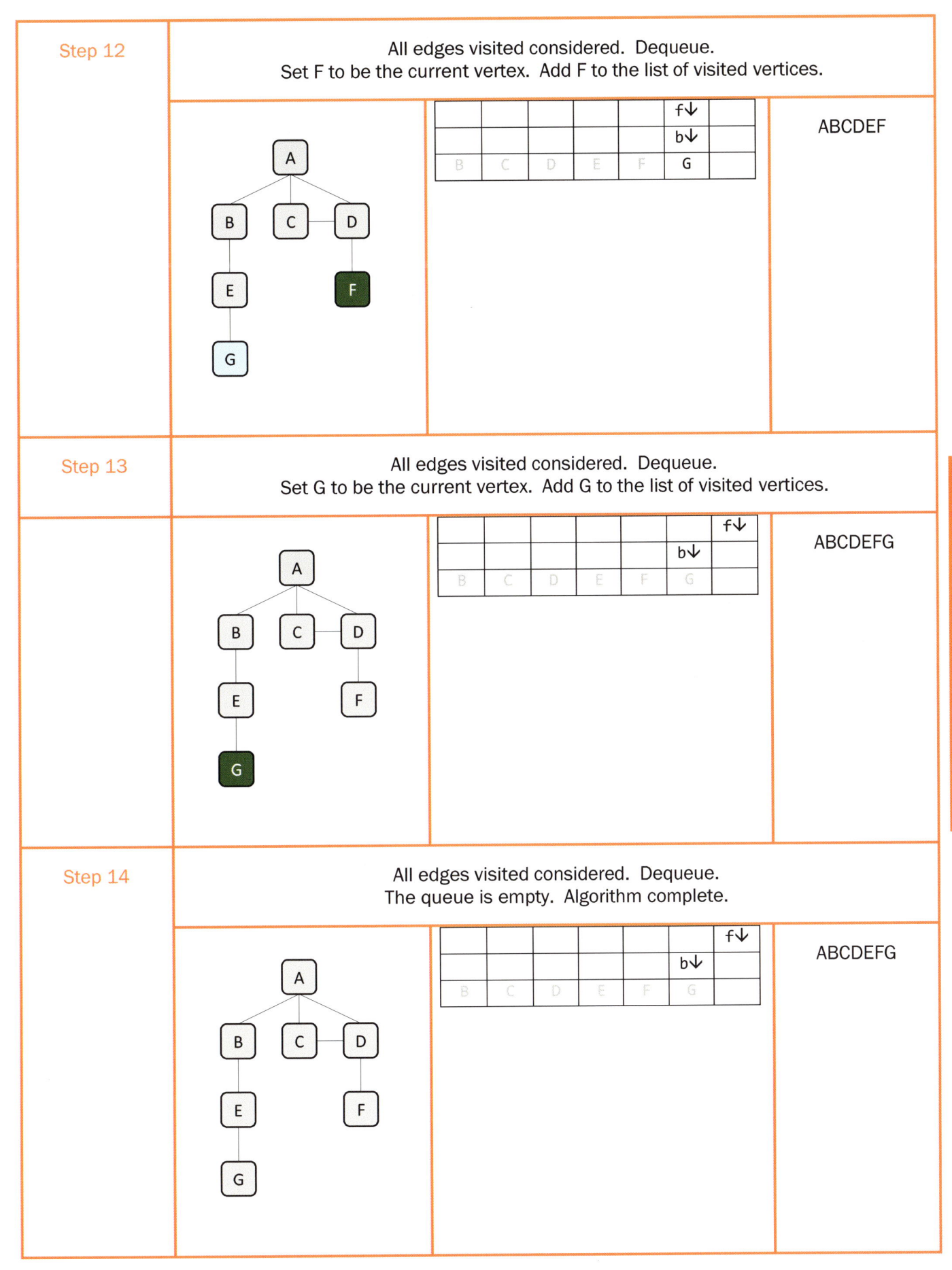

Step 12	All edges visited considered. Dequeue. Set F to be the current vertex. Add F to the list of visited vertices.		
	(tree: A—B,C,D; B—E; D—F [green]; E—G [light blue])	table with f↓ over G column, b↓ over G column; row: B C D E F G	ABCDEF

Step 13	All edges visited considered. Dequeue. Set G to be the current vertex. Add G to the list of visited vertices.		
	(tree: A—B,C,D; B—E; D—F; E—G [green])	table with f↓ over G, b↓ over F; row: B C D E F G	ABCDEFG

Step 14	All edges visited considered. Dequeue. The queue is empty. Algorithm complete.		
	(tree: A—B,C,D; B—E; D—F; E—G)	table with f↓ over G, b↓ over F; row: B C D E F G	ABCDEFG

Essential algorithms for A level Computer Science

It is worth noting that there is more than one valid output from a breadth-first search. This implementation examined the edges from A in the order B, C, D, from left to right. However, it would be perfectly valid to examine them in reverse order too, from right to left. To achieve this, the edges would need to be enqueued in reverse order.

Illustrated graph	Valid output 1	Valid output 2
	A B C D E F G This is the most common output shown in examples of this algorithm, so it is the one you should illustrate in exams unless the question specifically states otherwise.	A D C B F E G Reverse traversal.

Pseudocode for a breadth-first search

```
current_vertex = root
While current_vertex != Nothing
        If not visited.Contains(current_vertex) Then
                Visited.Add(current_vertex)
        End If
        For each edge in vertex
                If not visited.Contains(edge.vertex) Then
                        Queue.enqueue(edge.vertex)
                End If
        Next
        current_vertex = Queue.dequeue
End While
For each vertex in visited
        Output current_vertex
Next
```

Breadth-first search coded in Python

```python
class queue:

    class current_vertex:
        data = None
        pointer = None

    front_pointer = None
    back_pointer = None

    def enqueue(self,item):
        #Check queue overflow
        try:
            #Push the item
            new_current_vertex = queue.current_vertex()
            new_current_vertex.data = item
            #Empty queue
            if self.back_pointer == None:
                self.front_pointer = new_current_vertex
            else:
                self.back_pointer.pointer = new_current_vertex
            self.back_pointer = new_current_vertex
            return True
        except:
            return False

    def dequeue(self):
        #Check queue underflow
        if self.front_pointer != None:
            #Dequeue the item
            popped = self.front_pointer.data
            self.front_pointer = self.front_pointer.pointer
            #When the last item is dequeued reset the pointers
            if self.front_pointer == None:
                self.back_pointer = None
            return popped
        else:
            return None

#Main program starts here
graph = {"A":["B","C","D"],"B":["A","E"],"C":["A","D"],"D":["A","C","F"],"E":["B","G"],"F":["D"],"G":["E"]}
visited = []
q = queue()
current_vertex = "A"
while current_vertex != None:
    if not current_vertex in visited:
        visited.append(current_vertex)
```

Essential algorithms for A level Computer Science

```python
        for vertex in graph[current_vertex]:
            if not vertex in visited:
                q.enqueue(vertex)
        current_vertex = q.dequeue()
print(visited)
```

Breadth-first search coded in Visual Basic Console

```vb
Module Module1
    Public Class queue

        Private Class current_vertex
            Public data As String
            Public pointer As current_vertex
        End Class

        Private front_pointer As current_vertex
        Private back_pointer As current_vertex

        Function enqueue(item As String)
            'Check memory overflow
            Try
                'Push the item
                Dim new_current_vertex As New current_vertex
                new_current_vertex.data = item
                'Empty queue
                If IsNothing(back_pointer) Then
                    front_pointer = new_current_vertex
                Else
                    back_pointer.pointer = new_current_vertex
                End If
                back_pointer = new_current_vertex
                Return True
            Catch
                Return False
            End Try
        End Function

        Function dequeue()
            'Check queue underflow
            If Not IsNothing(front_pointer) Then
                'Dequeue the item
                Dim popped As String = front_pointer.data
                front_pointer = front_pointer.pointer
                'When the last item is dequeued reset the pointers
                If IsNothing(front_pointer) Then
                    back_pointer = Nothing
                End If
                Return popped
```

```vbnet
            Else
                Return Nothing
            End If
        End Function
    End Class

    Sub main()
        Dim graph = New Dictionary(Of String, List(Of String)) From {
            {"A", New List(Of String) From {"B", "C", "D"}},
            {"B", New List(Of String) From {"A", "E"}},
            {"C", New List(Of String) From {"A", "D"}},
            {"D", New List(Of String) From {"A", "C", "F"}},
            {"E", New List(Of String) From {"B", "G"}},
            {"F", New List(Of String) From {"D"}},
            {"G", New List(Of String) From {"E"}}
            }
        Dim visited As New List(Of String)
        Dim q As New queue
        Dim current_vertex As String = "A"
        Do While current_vertex <> Nothing
            If Not visited.Contains(current_vertex) Then
                visited.Add(current_vertex)
            End If
            For Each vertex In graph.Item(current_vertex)
                If Not visited.Contains(vertex) Then
                    q.enqueue(vertex)
                End If
            Next
            current_vertex = q.dequeue()
        Loop
        For Each current_vertex In visited
            Console.WriteLine(current_vertex)
        Next
        Console.ReadLine()
    End Sub
End Module
```

Depth-first search on a graph

Depth-first searches are used for pathfinding algorithms, operating system instruction scheduling, the order of formula recalculation in a spreadsheet, linkers and maze solution algorithms.

A depth-first search **requires the use of a stack** data structure.

Depth-first search in simple-structured English

1. Set a root vertex as the current vertex.
2. If the vertex has an edge that has not been visited:
    a. Push the linked vertex to the stack.
    b. Repeat from step 2 until all edges have been visited.
3. Add the current vertex to the list of visited vertices.
4. Pop the stack and set the item removed as the current vertex.
5. Repeat from step 2 until there are no vertices to visit.
6. Output all the visited vertices.

Depth-first search simplified with recursion

The above steps assume a user-defined stack with an iterative approach. However, it is also common to implement the algorithm using recursion. This simplifies the steps to:

1. Set a root vertex as the current vertex.
2. Output the vertex.
3. Add the current vertex to the list of visited vertices.
4. If the vertex has an edge that has not been visited:
    a. Follow the edge. The vertex becomes the current vertex.
    b. Repeat from step 2.

Depth-first search illustrated

If illustrations help you remember, this is how you can picture a breadth-first search on a graph:

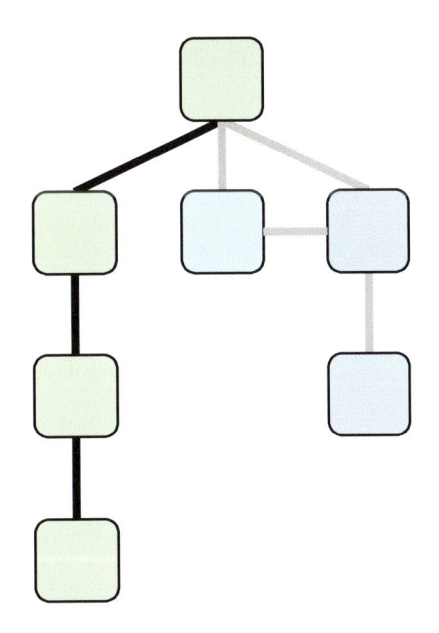

Traversing the graph

It is worth noting that there is more than one valid output from a depth-first search. You will typically see the left-most path being traversed first in mark schemes and other sources. However, it is perfectly valid to follow the right-most path first or to choose any random edge from a vertex to follow. In doing so, the results of the algorithm will be different, but nonetheless, it is still a depth-first search.

Providing the algorithm follows edges to the bottom of the structure for any vertex, the output is valid, as shown below.

Illustrated graph	Valid output 1	Valid output 2	Other valid outputs
	A B E G C D F	A D F C B E G	A C D F B E G
	This is the most common output shown in examples of this algorithm, so it is the one you should illustrate in exams unless the question specifically states otherwise.	Reverse traversal.	A C B E G D F
			A D F B E G C

Essential algorithms for A level Computer Science

Stepping through the depth-first search using iteration and a user-defined stack

There are many different approaches to the depth-first search algorithm. Each one uses a stack in different ways to achieve an output. Using iteration as shown below, each vertex linked to an edge is added to the stack before moving to the next vertex. Later in the chapter, we will contrast this by using a recursive technique where we rely on the call stack only.

	Graph	Stack	Visited
Step 1	Start at a root vertex. Add A to the list of visited vertices.		
	(graph with A at root; children B, C, D; E under B; F under D; G under E)	(empty stack)	A
Step 2	Push D.		
	(same graph, D highlighted)	→ D	A

54

Step 3	Push C.		
	(tree with C highlighted)	→ C D	A

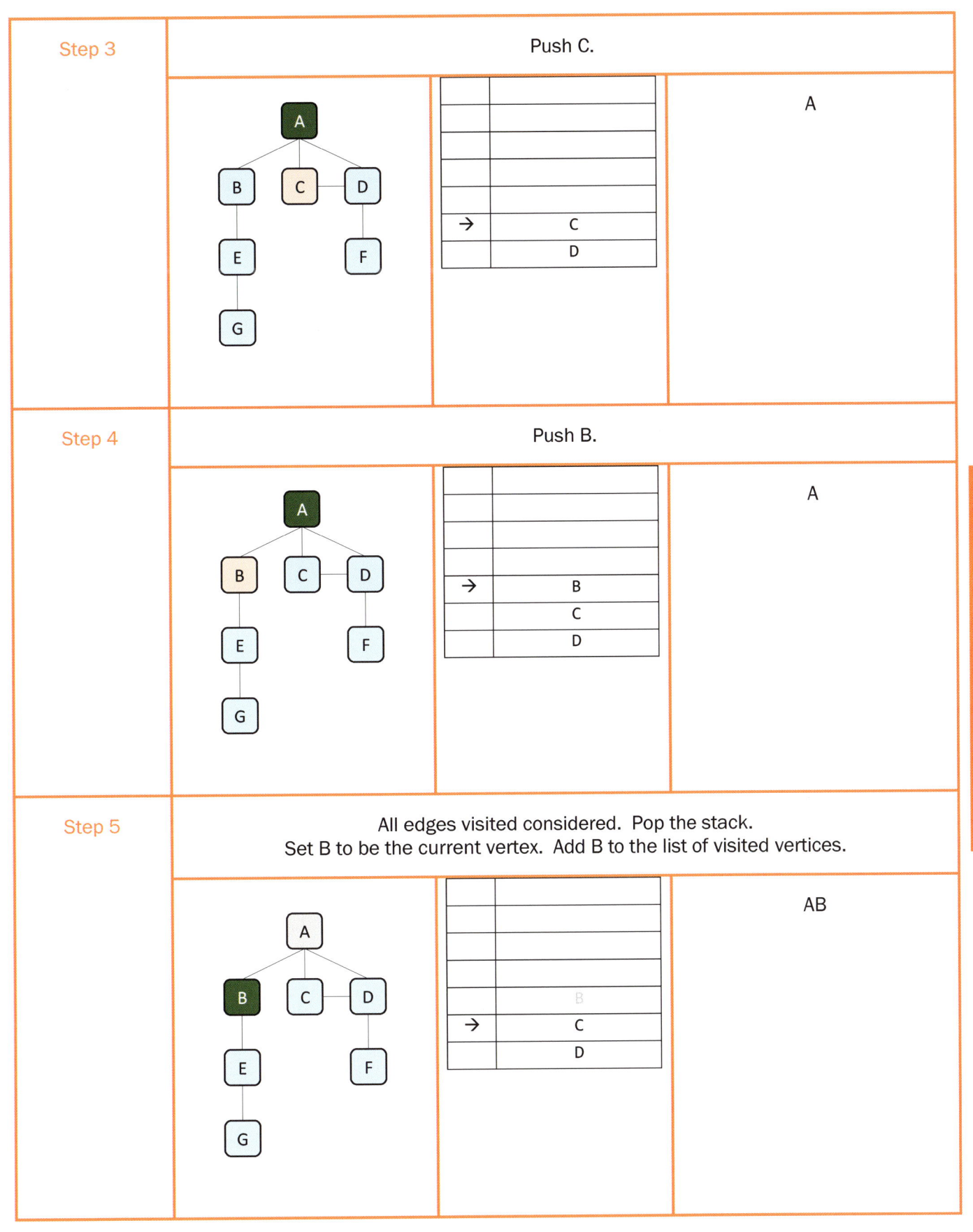

Step 4	Push B.		
	(tree with B highlighted)	→ B C D	A

Step 5	All edges visited considered. Pop the stack. Set B to be the current vertex. Add B to the list of visited vertices.		
	(tree with B highlighted green)	B → C D	AB

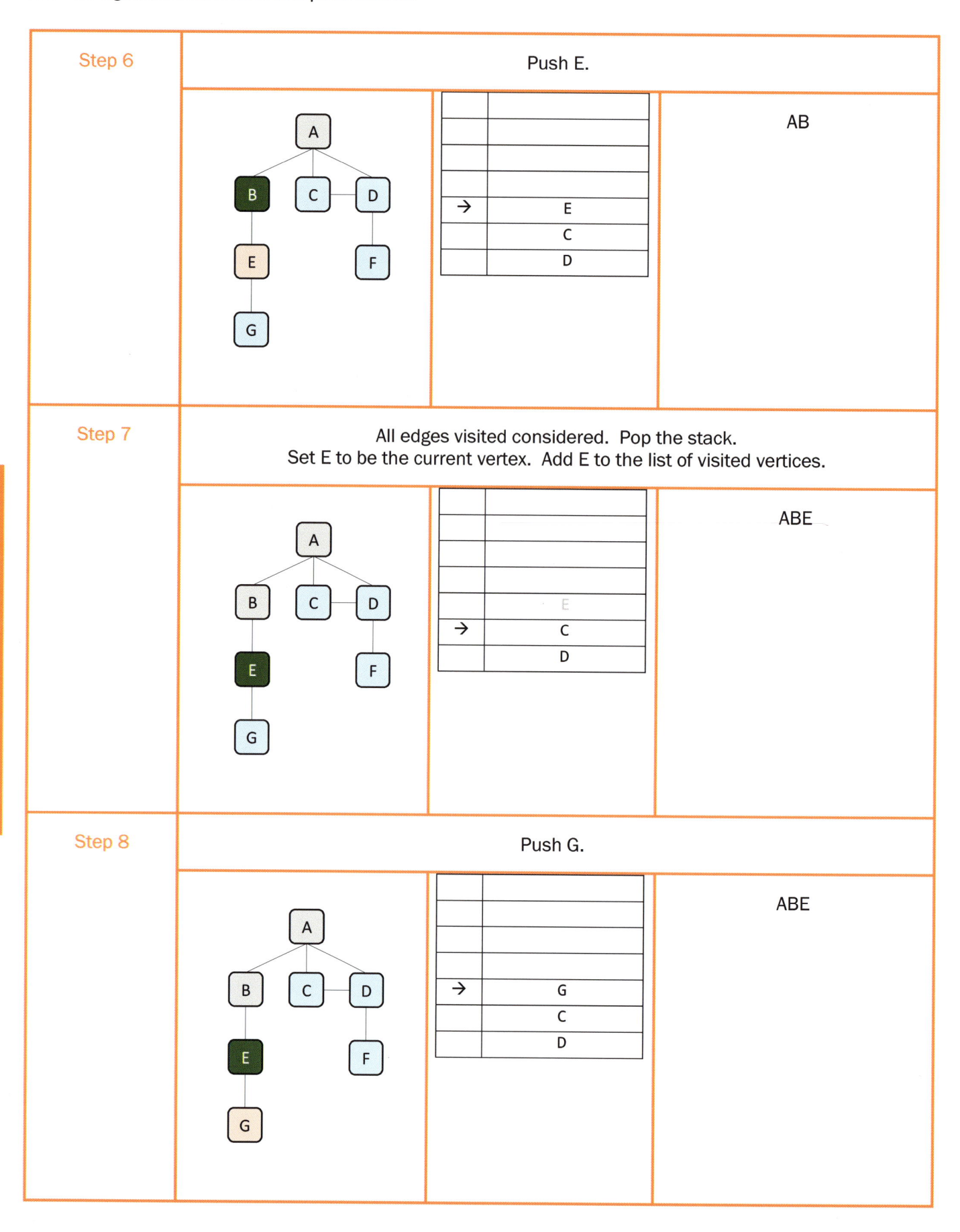

Essential algorithms for A level Computer Science

Step 6	Push E.		
	(tree: A-B,C,D; B-E; D-F; E-G; B highlighted dark, E highlighted light)	→ E C D	AB

Step 7	All edges visited considered. Pop the stack. Set E to be the current vertex. Add E to the list of visited vertices.		
	(tree: A-B,C,D; B-E; D-F; E-G; E highlighted dark)	~~E~~ → C D	ABE

Step 8	Push G.		
	(tree: A-B,C,D; B-E; D-F; E-G; E highlighted dark, G highlighted light)	→ G C D	ABE

Higher order data structures

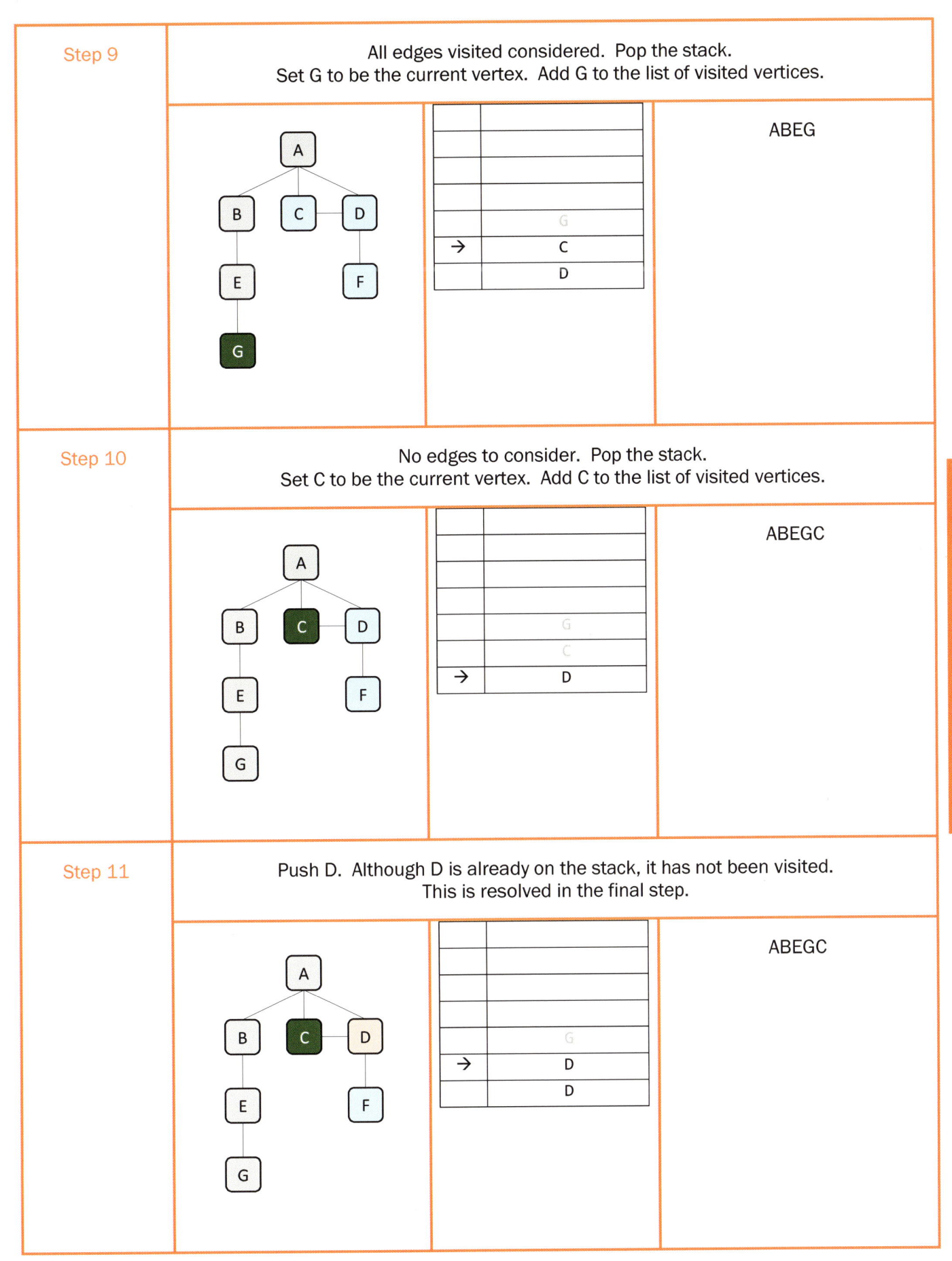

Step 9	All edges visited considered. Pop the stack. Set G to be the current vertex. Add G to the list of visited vertices.		
	Graph: A connected to B, C, D; B connected to E; E connected to G (highlighted); D connected to F.	Stack: (empty), G, → C, D	ABEG

Step 10	No edges to consider. Pop the stack. Set C to be the current vertex. Add C to the list of visited vertices.		
	Graph: A connected to B, C (highlighted), D; B connected to E; E connected to G; D connected to F.	Stack: (empty), G, C, → D	ABEGC

Step 11	Push D. Although D is already on the stack, it has not been visited. This is resolved in the final step.		
	Graph: A connected to B, C (highlighted), D (highlighted light); B connected to E; E connected to G; D connected to F.	Stack: (empty), G, → D, D	ABEGC

57

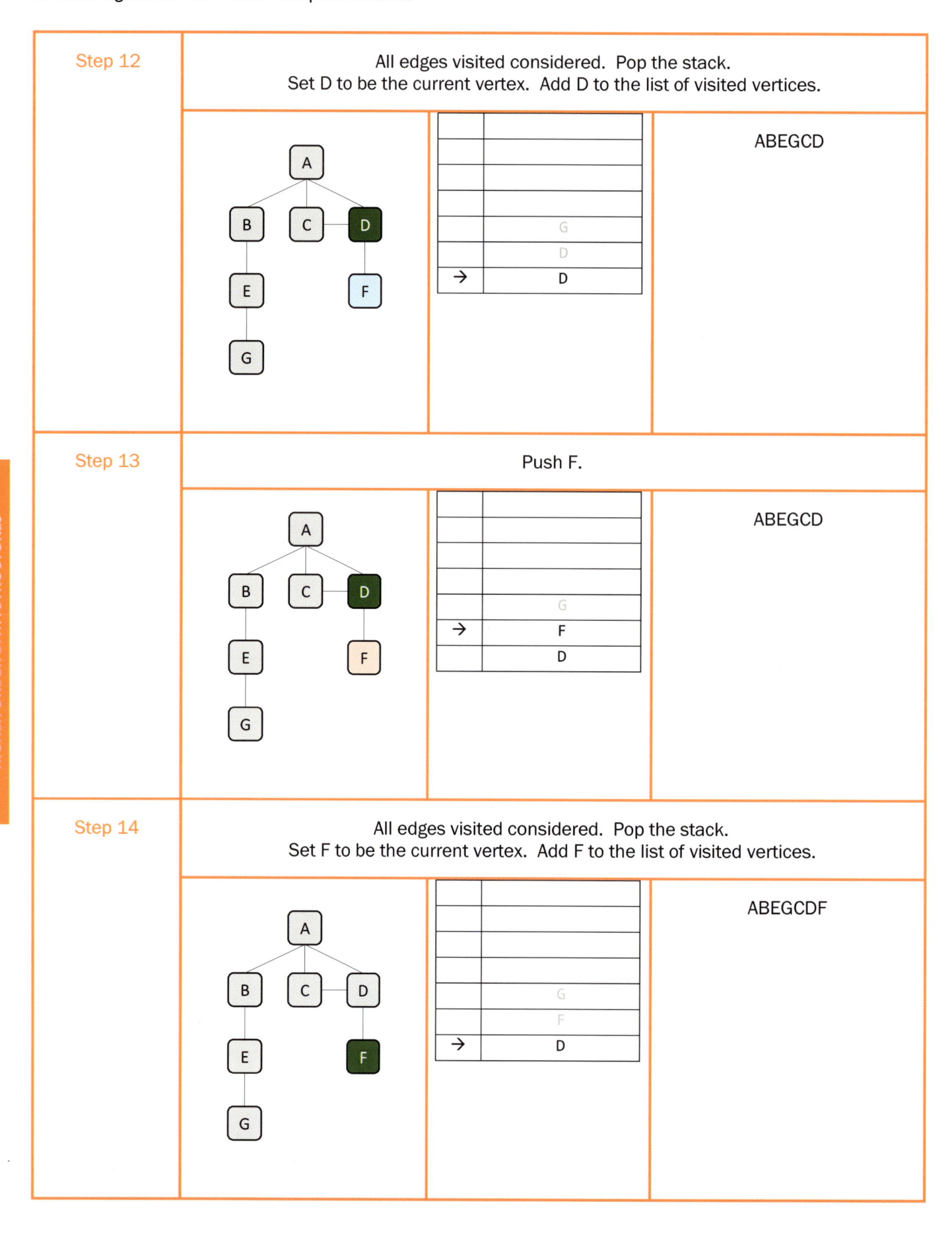

Essential algorithms for A level Computer Science

Step 12	All edges visited considered. Pop the stack. Set D to be the current vertex. Add D to the list of visited vertices.		
	Graph with A at top connected to B, C, D. B connects to E. E connects to G. D connects to F. D highlighted.	Stack: G, D, → D	ABEGCD

Step 13	Push F.		
	Graph with A at top connected to B, C, D. B connects to E. E connects to G. D connects to F. F highlighted.	Stack: G, → F, D	ABEGCD

Step 14	All edges visited considered. Pop the stack. Set F to be the current vertex. Add F to the list of visited vertices.		
	Graph with A at top connected to B, C, D. B connects to E. E connects to G. D connects to F. F highlighted (dark).	Stack: G, F, → D	ABEGCDF

58

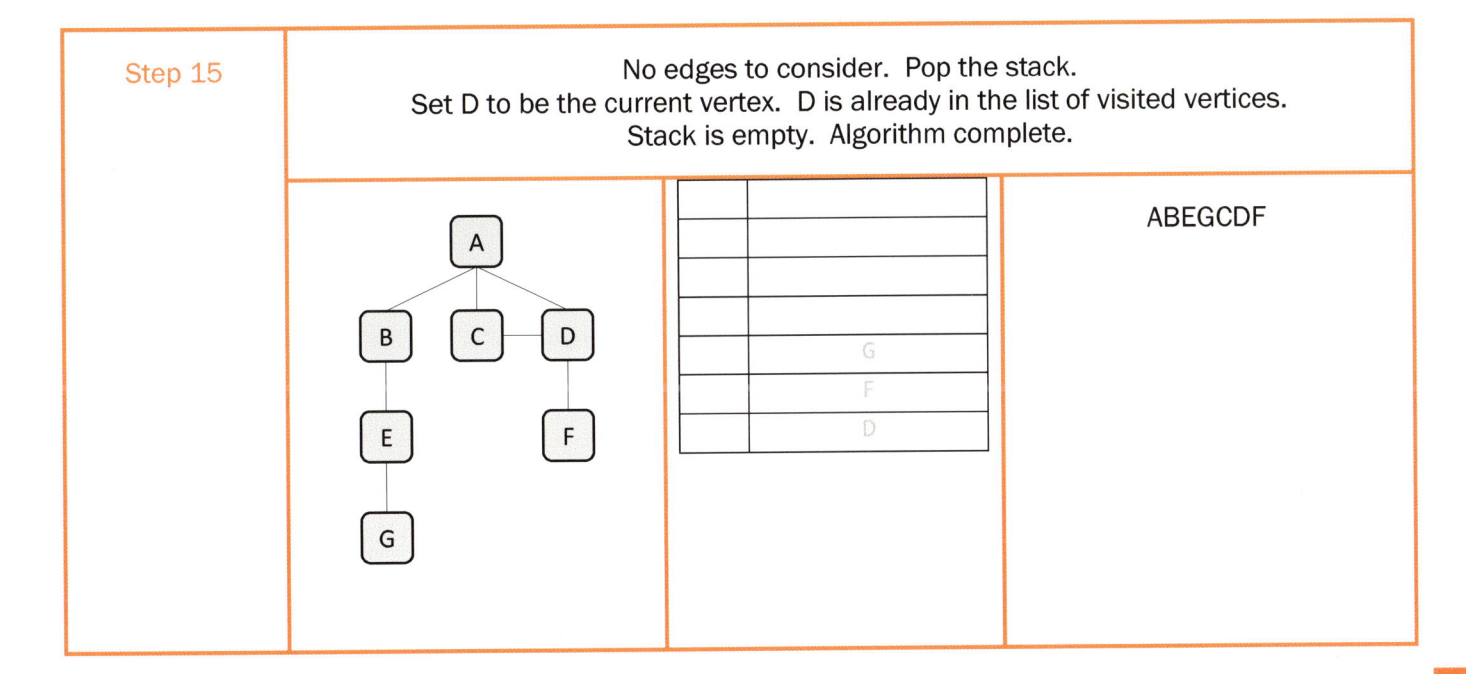

Step 15	No edges to consider. Pop the stack. Set D to be the current vertex. D is already in the list of visited vertices. Stack is empty. Algorithm complete.		
	A — B, C, D; B — E; E — G; D — F	G / F / D	ABEGCDF

Did you know?

All algorithms with repeating instructions can be coded using iteration instead of recursion. It is usually the best choice because iterative algorithms execute within a defined memory space and are not reliant on free space in the call stack. However, it is often easier to program when writing recursive algorithms — and more readable code is created. It may even be possible to make use of parallel processing to maximise efficiency.

Essential algorithms for A level Computer Science

Stepping through the depth-first search using recursion and the call stack

Although the use of a user-defined stack delivers the correct output, using only the procedure call stack with recursion is somewhat simpler. This approach is most likely to feature in mark schemes of depth-first search-related questions.

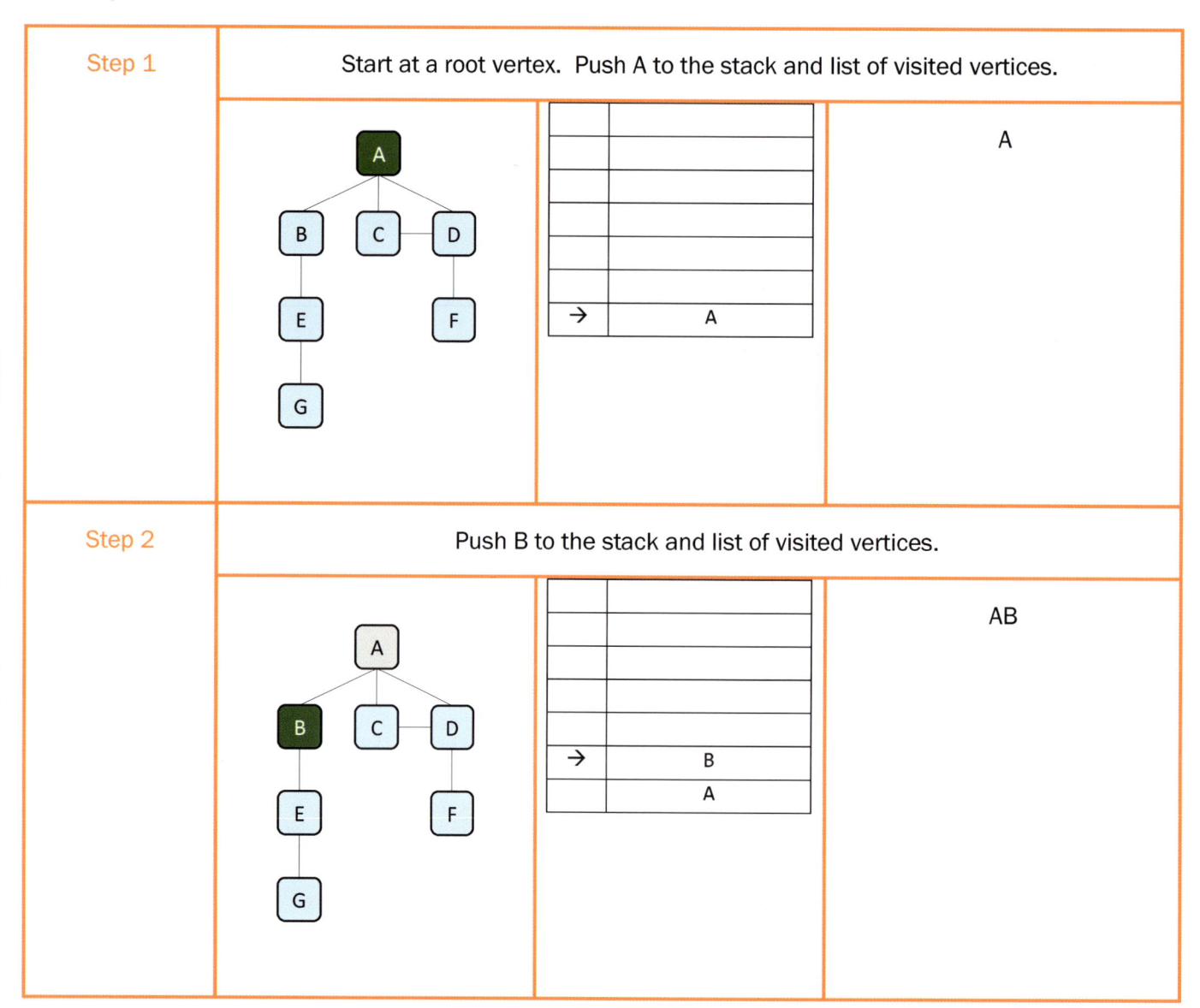

Step 1	Start at a root vertex. Push A to the stack and list of visited vertices.		
	Graph with A highlighted (root), connected to B, C, D; B connects to E; E connects to G; D connects to F.	Stack: → A	Visited: A

Step 2	Push B to the stack and list of visited vertices.		
	Graph with B highlighted; same structure.	Stack: → B, A	Visited: AB

60

Higher order data structures

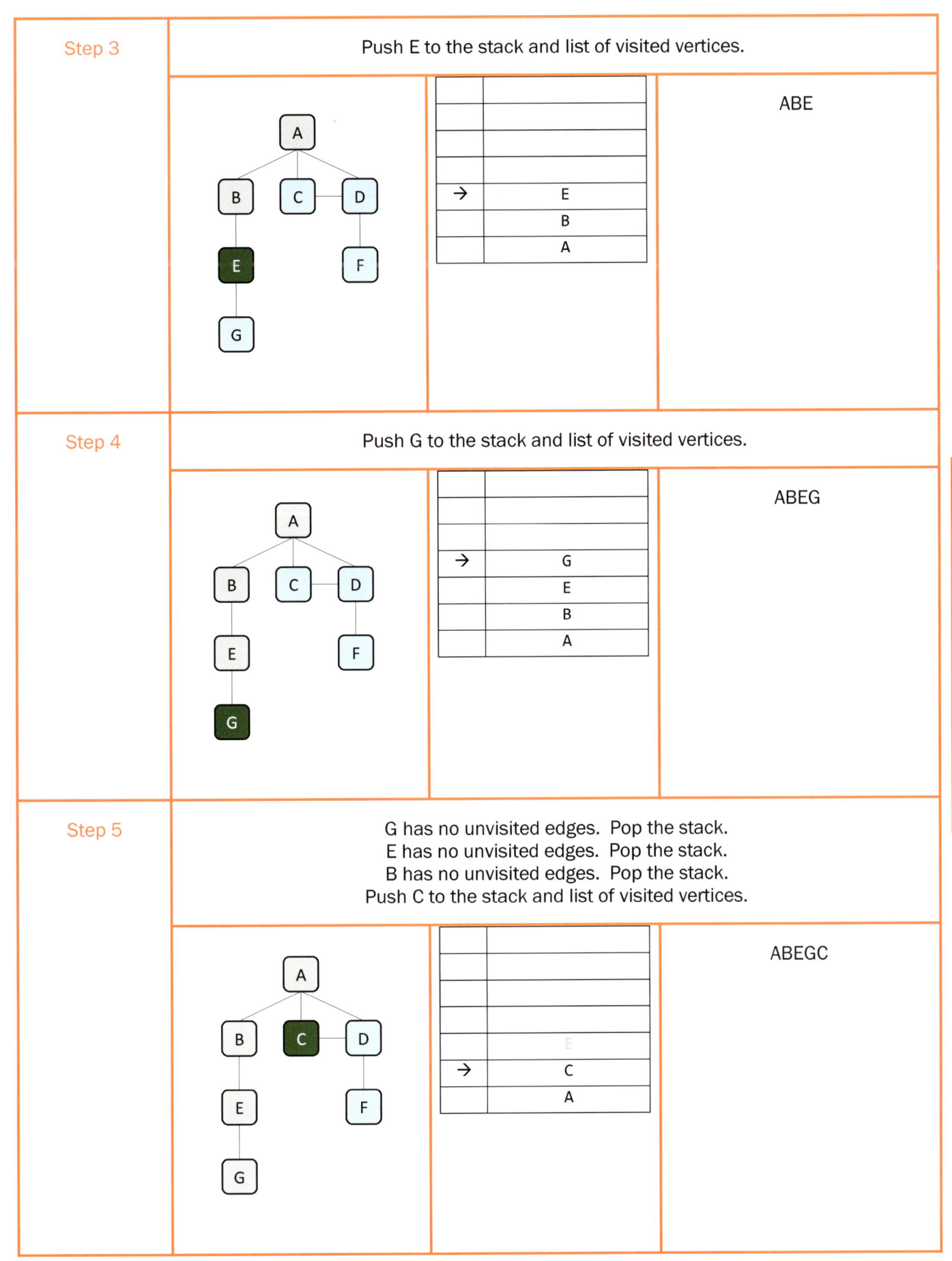

Step 3	Push E to the stack and list of visited vertices.		
	(graph with E highlighted)	→ E / B / A	ABE

Step 4	Push G to the stack and list of visited vertices.		
	(graph with G highlighted)	→ G / E / B / A	ABEG

Step 5	G has no unvisited edges. Pop the stack. E has no unvisited edges. Pop the stack. B has no unvisited edges. Pop the stack. Push C to the stack and list of visited vertices.		
	(graph with C highlighted)	E / → C / A	ABEGC

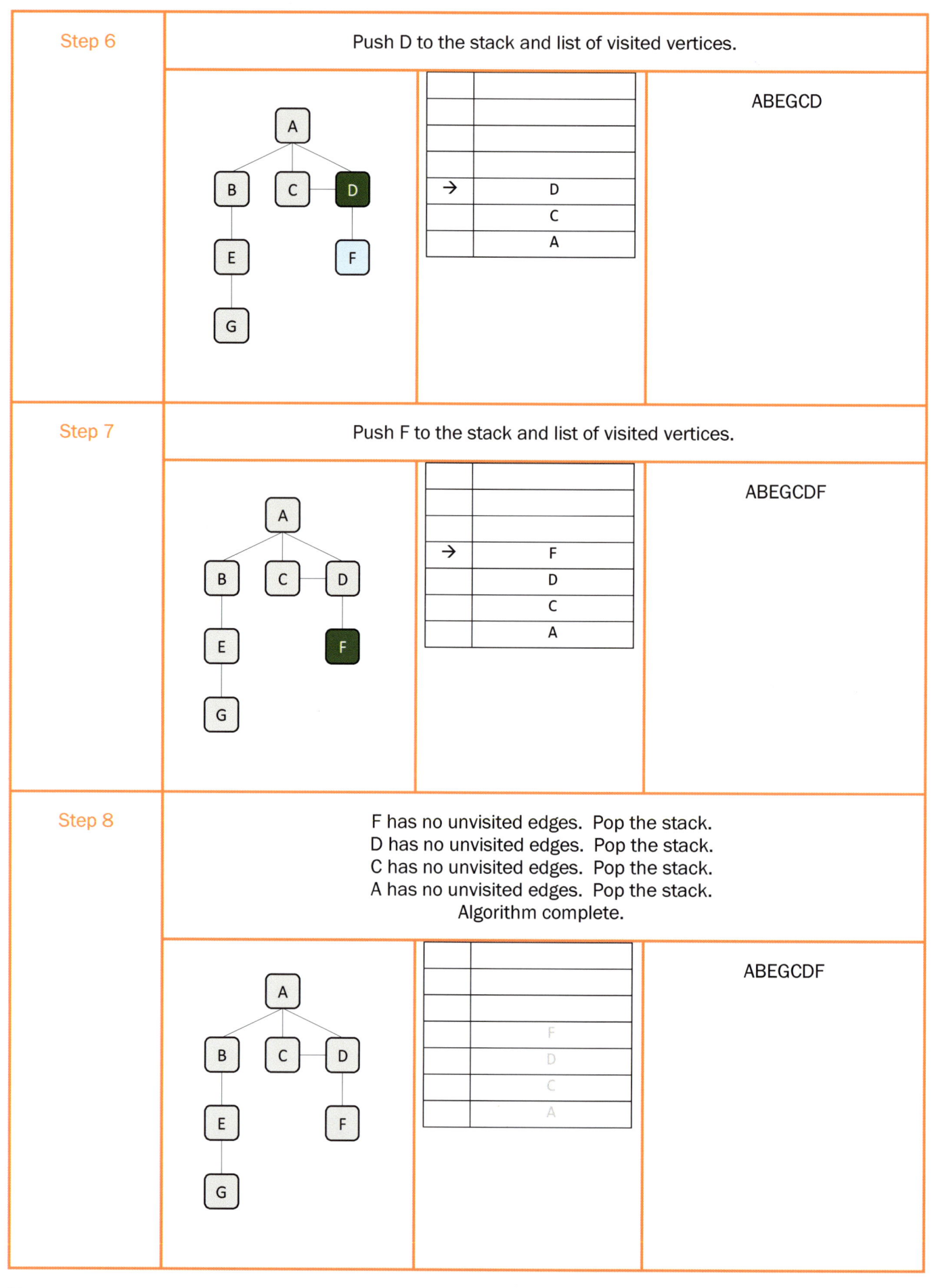

Essential algorithms for A level Computer Science

Step 6	Push D to the stack and list of visited vertices.		
	Tree with A at root; children B, C, D (D highlighted dark); B has child E; E has child G; D has child F (light blue)	Stack: → D / C / A	ABEGCD

Step 7	Push F to the stack and list of visited vertices.		
	Tree with A at root; children B, C, D; B has child E; E has child G; D has child F (highlighted dark)	Stack: → F / D / C / A	ABEGCDF

Step 8	F has no unvisited edges. Pop the stack. D has no unvisited edges. Pop the stack. C has no unvisited edges. Pop the stack. A has no unvisited edges. Pop the stack. Algorithm complete.		
	Tree with A at root; children B, C, D; B has child E; E has child G; D has child F	Stack empty (F, D, C, A faded)	ABEGCDF

Pseudocode for a depth-first search

```
current_vertex = root
While current_vertex != Nothing
        If not visited.Contains(current_vertex) Then
              Visited.Add(current_vertex)
        End If
        For each edge in vertex
              If not visited.Contains(edge.vertex) Then
                    Stack.push(edge.vertex)
              End If
        Next
        current_vertex = Stack.pop
End While
For each vertex in visited
        Output current_vertex
Next
```

Depth-first search coded in Python using iteration

```python
class stack:

    class current_vertex:
        data = None
        pointer = None

    stack_pointer = None

    def push(self,item):
        #Check stack overflow
        try:
            #Push the item
            new_current_vertex = stack.current_vertex()
            new_current_vertex.data = item
            new_current_vertex.pointer = self.stack_pointer
            self.stack_pointer = new_current_vertex
            return True
        except:
            return False

    def pop(self):
        #Check stack underflow
        if self.stack_pointer != None:
            #Pop the item
            popped = self.stack_pointer.data
            self.stack_pointer = self.stack_pointer.pointer
            return popped
        else:
            return None
```

```python
#Main program starts here
graph = {"A":["B","C","D"],"B":["A","E"],"C":["A","D"],"D":["A","C","F"],"E":["B","G"],"F":["D"],"G":["E"]}
visited = []
s = stack()
current_vertex = "A"
while current_vertex != None:
    for vertex in reversed(graph[current_vertex]):
        if not vertex in visited:
            s.push(vertex)
    if not current_vertex in visited:
        visited.append(current_vertex)
    current_vertex = s.pop()
print(visited)
```

Depth-first search coded in Python using recursion

```python
def dfs(graph, current_vertex):
    visited.append(current_vertex)
    for vertex in graph[current_vertex]:
        if not vertex in visited:
            dfs(graph, vertex)

#Main program starts here
graph = {"A":["B","C","D"],"B":["A","E"],"C":["A","D"],"D":["A","C","F"],"E":["B","G"],"F":["D"],"G":["E"]}
visited = []
dfs(graph,"A")
print(visited)
```

Depth-first search coded in Visual Basic Console using iteration

```vb
Module Module1
    Public Class stack

        Private Class current_vertex
            Public data As String
            Public pointer As current_vertex
        End Class

        Private stack_pointer As current_vertex

        Function push(item As String)
            'Check memory overflow
            Try
                'Push the item
                Dim new_current_vertex As New current_vertex
                new_current_vertex.data = item
                new_current_vertex.pointer = stack_pointer
                stack_pointer = new_current_vertex
                Return True
            Catch
                Return False
            End Try
        End Function

        Function pop()
            'Check stack underflow
            If Not IsNothing(stack_pointer) Then
                'Pop the item
                Dim popped As String = stack_pointer.data
                stack_pointer = stack_pointer.pointer
                Return popped
            Else
                Return Nothing
            End If
        End Function
    End Class

    Sub main()
        Dim graph = New Dictionary(Of String, List(Of String)) From {
            {"A", New List(Of String) From {"B", "C", "D"}},
            {"B", New List(Of String) From {"E", "A"}},
            {"C", New List(Of String) From {"A", "D"}},
            {"D", New List(Of String) From {"A", "C", "F"}},
            {"E", New List(Of String) From {"B", "G"}},
            {"F", New List(Of String) From {"D"}},
            {"G", New List(Of String) From {"E"}}
            }
```

Essential algorithms for A level Computer Science

```vbnet
        Dim visited As New List(Of String)
        Dim edges As List(Of String)
        Dim s As New stack
        Dim current_vertex As String = "A"
        Do While current_vertex <> Nothing
            edges = graph.Item(current_vertex)
            edges.Reverse()
            For Each vertex In edges
                If Not visited.Contains(vertex) Then
                    s.push(vertex)
                End If
            Next
            If Not visited.Contains(current_vertex) Then
                visited.Add(current_vertex)
            End If
            current_vertex = s.pop()
        Loop
        For Each current_vertex In visited
            Console.WriteLine(current_vertex)
        Next
        Console.ReadLine()
    End Sub
End Module
```

Depth-first search coded in Visual Basic Console using recursion

```vbnet
Module Module1
    Dim visited As New List(Of String)

    Sub dfs(graph As Dictionary(Of String, List(Of String)), current_vertex As String)
        visited.Add(current_vertex)
        Dim edges As List(Of String) = graph.Item(current_vertex)
        For Each vertex In edges
            If Not visited.Contains(vertex) Then
                dfs(graph, vertex)
            End If
        Next
    End Sub

    Sub main()
        Dim graph = New Dictionary(Of String, List(Of String)) From {
            {"A", New List(Of String) From {"B", "C", "D"}},
            {"B", New List(Of String) From {"E", "A"}},
            {"C", New List(Of String) From {"A", "D"}},
            {"D", New List(Of String) From {"A", "C", "F"}},
            {"E", New List(Of String) From {"B", "G"}},
            {"F", New List(Of String) From {"D"}},
            {"G", New List(Of String) From {"E"}}
            }
```

```
        dfs(graph, "A")
        For Each current_vertex In visited
            Console.WriteLine(current_vertex)
        Next
        Console.ReadLine()
    End Sub
End Module
```

Efficiency of a graph

Space complexity of a graph

Object implementation	Array implementation
O(n) Linear	O(1) Constant

Although the examples presented in this chapter have used a static dictionary, a graph is considered a dynamic data structure. When implemented using object-oriented techniques, its memory footprint grows and shrinks as data is added and deleted from the structure. Using only as much memory as needed is the most efficient way of implementing a graph.

When implementing a graph as an array, the memory footprint remains constant, but operations such as adding new vertices would require the matrix to be recreated. Graphs would not be stored using arrays if this were a requirement, as the operation would be too slow. Therefore, we can assume a constant space complexity at the expense of data structure flexibility.

Time complexity of operations on a graph

Operation	Object implementation Adjacency list	Array implementation Adjacency matrix
Storing the graph	$O(V+E)$ Linear	$O(V^2)$ Polynomial
Add a vertex	$O(1)$ Constant	$O(V^2)$ Polynomial
Add an edge	$O(1)$ Constant	$O(1)$ Constant

Remove a vertex	O(E) Linear	O(V²) Polynomial
Remove an edge	O(V) Linear	O(1) Constant

When expressing the time complexity of operations on a graph, V represents the number of vertices and E represents the number of edges. Storing a graph using object-oriented techniques is far superior to using an array in most cases — the only exception being removing edges and checking the adjacency of two vertices.

Both of these operations are constant — O(1) — with an adjacency matrix, as you can immediately return an element of an index in an array.

However, they are linear — O(V) — with an object-oriented approach since it is necessary to follow the edges to find a particular vertex.

Efficiency of a breadth and depth-first search

Best case	Average case	Worst case
O(1) Constant	O(V+E) Linear	O(V²) Polynomial

The breadth-first search can be used to find a single vertex in the structure or output all the data stored in it. At best, the graph contains just one vertex, so it can be found immediately — O(1) — but if that were the case, there wouldn't be any point in having the data structure at all.

Usually, many vertices need to be visited, so it is of linear complexity — O(V+E), where V represents the number of vertices and E the number of edges. A full traversal requires visiting every vertex and considering every edge from the vertex. Therefore, it has polynomial complexity: O(V²). Notice the nested loop in the iteration and recursion examples, which are both an indication of polynomial complexity.

Linked list

A linked list is a data structure that provides a foundation upon which other data structures can be built such as stacks, queues, graphs and trees. A linked list is constructed from nodes and pointers. A start pointer identifies the first node. Each node contains data and a pointer to the next node in the linked list. Many programming languages support lists in addition to arrays. Data in lists can be stored anywhere in memory, with pointers indicating the address of the next item in the structure.

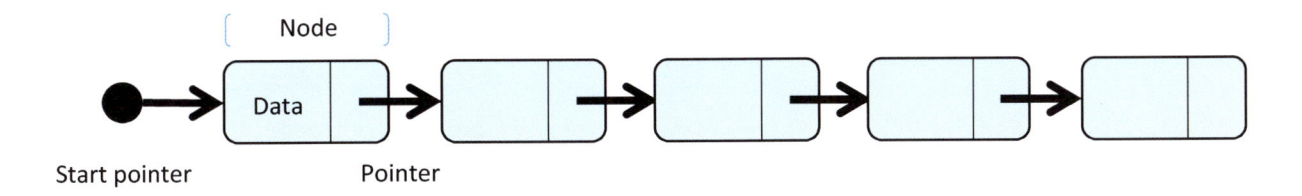

While a linked list can be implemented using a static array, its true benefit becomes evident when implemented using object-oriented techniques.

Arrays, being static data structures, are stored contiguously in memory, requiring the use of an index register to determine where an index of an array is in memory from a base address. With a linked list implemented using objects, any available memory address can be used to store data. It does not need to be adjacent, as each node points to the next in the structure. The memory footprint of the data structure is not determined at compile time and can change dynamically at run-time, referred to as a **dynamic data structure**.

By adding an extra pointer, nodes can point to the previous and next items, known as a doubly linked list:

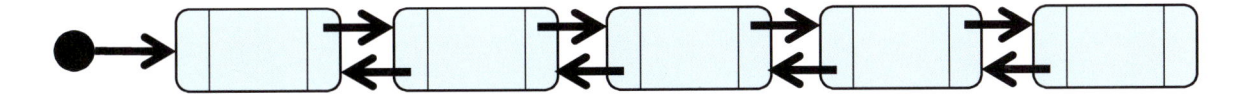

By making the last node point to the first node, a circular linked list can be created:

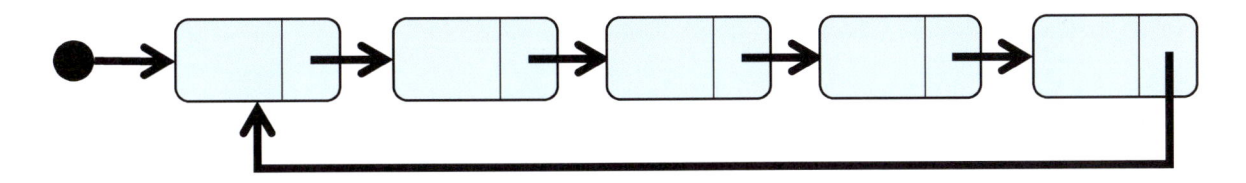

A circular linked list can also have an additional pointer for each node pointing to the previous item, turning it into a doubly circular linked list.

Essential algorithms for A level Computer Science

Applications of a linked list

Linked lists can be used to store process blocks in a ready state for operating systems managing a processor, image viewers moving between previous and next images, music players storing tracks in a playlist or navigating backwards and forwards in a web browser. Linked lists could also be used for hash table collision resolution as an overflow or maintaining a file allocation table of linked clusters on a secondary storage medium such as a hard disk.

Operations on a linked list

Typical operations that can be performed on a linked list include:

- Add: adds a node to the linked list
- Delete: removes a node from the linked list
- Next: moves to the next item in the list
- Previous: moves to the previous item in a doubly linked list
- Traverse: a linear search through the linked list

Craig'n'Dave videos

https://www.craigndave.org/algorithm-linked-list

Adding an item to a linked list in simple-structured English

1. Check there is free memory for a new node. Output an error if not.
2. Create a new node and insert data into it.
3. If the linked list is empty:
   a. The new node becomes the first item. Create a start pointer to it.
4. If the new node should be placed before the first node:
   a. The new node becomes the first node. Change the start pointer to it.
   b. The new node points to the second node.
5. If the new node is to be placed inside the linked list:
   a. Start at the first node.
   b. If the data in the current node is less than the value of the new node:
      i. Follow the pointer to the next node.

ii. Repeat from step 5b until the correct position is found or the end of the linked list is reached.

c. The new node is set to point where the previous node pointed.

d. The previous node is set to point to the new node.

Adding an item to a linked list illustrated

If illustrations help you remember, this is how you can picture adding an item to a linked list:

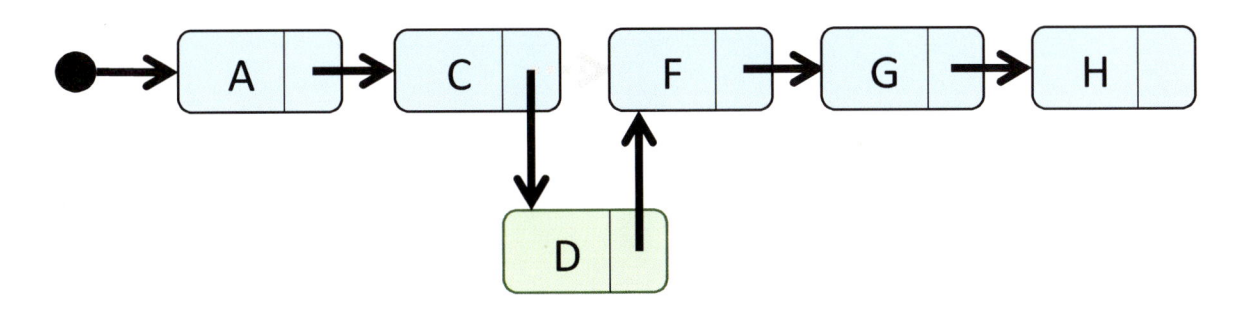

The assumption here is that we are maintaining an ordered list. If that is not necessary, a new node can simply be added to the end of the list.

Pseudocode for adding an item to a linked list

```
If not memoryfull Then
        new_node = New Node
        current_node = start_pointer
        If current_node == Null Then
                new_node.pointer = Null
                start_pointer = new_node
        Else
                If item < current_node.data Then
                        start_pointer = new_node
                        new_node.pointer = current_node
                Else
                        While current_node != Null And item < current_node.data
                                previous_node = current_node
                                current_node = current_node.pointer
                        End While
                        new_node.pointer = previous_node.pointer
                        previous_node.pointer = new_node
                End If
        End If
End If
```

Deleting an item from a linked list in simple-structured English

1. Check if the linked list is empty and output an error if there is no start node.
2. If the first item is the item to delete, set the start pointer to nothing.
3. If the item to delete is inside the linked list:
    a. Start at the first node.
    b. If the current node is the item to delete:
        i. The previous node's pointer is set to point to the next node.
    c. Follow the pointer to the next node.
    d. Repeat from step 3b until the item is found or the end of the linked list is reached.

Deleting an item to a linked list illustrated

If illustrations help you remember, this is how you can picture deleting an item from a linked list:

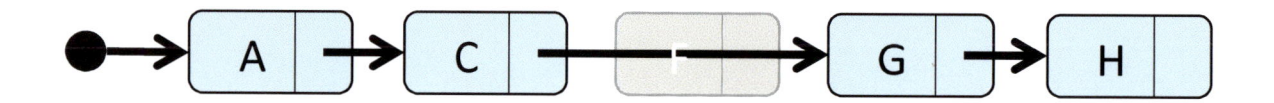

Pseudocode for deleting an item from a linked list

```
current_node = start_pointer
If current_node != Null Then
        If item == current_node.data Then
                start_pointer = current_node.pointer
        Else
                While current_node != Null And item != current_node.data
                        previous_node = current_node
                        current_node = current_node.pointer
                End While
                previous_node.pointer = current_node.pointer
        End If
End If
```

Traversing a linked list in simple-structured English

1. Check if the linked list is empty.
2. Start at the node the start pointer is pointing to.
3. Output the item.
4. Follow the pointer to the next node.
5. Repeat from step 3 until the end of the linked list is reached.

Pseudocode for traversing a linked list

```
current_node = start_pointer
If current_node != Null Then
      While current_node != Null
            Output current_node
            current_node = current_node.pointer
      End While
End If
```

Did you know?

A linked list is actually just a list. Many programming languages now support linked lists as a fundamental data structure, but they may implement them internally as arrays.

Searching a linked list with commands such as `if x in list` abstracts the actual process happening internally, which may be a linear search.

Essential algorithms for A level Computer Science

Linked list coded in Python

```python
class linkedlist:

    class node:
        data = None
        pointer = None

    start = None

    def add(self,item):
        #Check memory overflow
        try:
            new_node = linkedlist.node()
            new_node.data = item
            current_node = self.start
            #List is empty
            if current_node == None:
                new_node.pointer = None
                self.start = new_node
            else:
                #Item becomes the new start item
                if item < current_node.data:
                    self.start = new_node
                    new_node.pointer = current_node
                else:
                    #Find correct position in the list
                    while current_node != None and current_node.data < item:
                        previous_node = current_node
                        current_node = current_node.pointer
                    new_node.pointer = previous_node.pointer
                    previous_node.pointer = new_node
            return True
        except:
            return False

    def delete(self,item):
        current_node = self.start
        #Check the list is not empty
        if current_node != None:
            #Item is the start node
            if item == current_node.data:
                self.start = current_node.pointer
            else:
                #Find item in the list
                while current_node != None and item != current_node.data:
                    previous = current_node
                    current_node = current_node.pointer
                previous.pointer = current_node.pointer
```

```python
    def output(self):
        items = []
        current_node = self.start
        if current_node != None:
            #Visit each node
            while current_node != None:
                items.append(current_node.data)
                current_node = current_node.pointer
        return items
```

Adding items to a linked list object in Python

```python
items = ["Florida","Georgia","Delaware","Alabama","California"]
l = linkedlist()
for index in range(0,len(items)):
    l.add(items[index])
```

Deleting items from a linked list object in Python

```python
l.delete("Florida")
```

Outputting items from a linked list object in Python

```python
print(l.output())
```

> **Did you know?**
>
> Although many programming languages today support commands that automatically add, delete, search and sort data in a list, if you are asked to write pseudocode for the algorithms in an exam, you must assume they are not built into the language.
>
> For example, if asked to show the steps of a sorting algorithm, do not write "`list.sort()`" even though this works in languages such as Python.

Essential algorithms for A level Computer Science

Linked list coded in Visual Basic Console

```vb
Module Module1
    Public Class linkedlist

        Private Class node
            Public data As String
            Public pointer As node
        End Class

        Private start As node

        Function add(item As String)
            'Check memory overflow
            Try
                Dim new_node As New node
                new_node.data = item
                Dim current_node As node = start
                'List is empty
                If IsNothing(current_node) Then
                    new_node.pointer = Nothing
                    start = new_node
                Else
                    'Item becomes the new start item
                    If item < current_node.data Then
                        start = new_node
                        new_node.pointer = current_node
                    Else
                        'Find correct position in the list
                        Dim previous_node As node
                        Do While Not IsNothing(current_node) AndAlso current_node.data < item
                            previous_node = current_node
                            current_node = current_node.pointer
                        Loop
                        new_node.pointer = previous_node.pointer
                        previous_node.pointer = new_node
                    End If
                End If
                Return True
            Catch
                Return False
            End Try
        End Function

        Sub delete(item As String)
            Dim new_node As New node
            Dim current_node As node = start
            'Check the list is not empty
            If Not IsNothing(current_node) Then
```

```vb
                'Item is the start node
                If item = current_node.data Then
                    start = current_node.pointer
                Else
                    'Find item in the list
                    Dim previous_node As node
                    previous_node = current_node
                    Do While Not IsNothing(current_node) AndAlso item <> current_node.data
                        previous_node = current_node
                        current_node = current_node.pointer
                    Loop
                    Previous_node.pointer = current_node.pointer
                End If
            End If
        End Sub

        Function output()
            Dim items As New List(Of String)
            Dim current_node As node = start
            If Not IsNothing(current_node) Then
                'Visit each node
                Do While Not IsNothing(current_node)
                    items.Add(current_node.data)
                    current_node = current_node.pointer
                Loop
            End If
            Return items
        End Function
    End Class

End Module
```

Adding items to a linked list object in Visual Basic Console

```vb
Dim items() As String = {"Florida", "Georgia", "Delaware", "Alabama", "California"}
Dim l As New linkedlist
For index = 0 To items.Length - 1
    l.add(items(index))
Next
```

Deleting items from a linked list object in Visual Basic Console

```vb
l.delete("Florida")
```

Outputting items from a linked list object in Visual Basic Console

```vb
Dim output As New List(Of String)
output = l.output()
For Each item In output
    Console.WriteLine(item)
Next
```

Efficiency of a linked list

Space complexity of a linked list

Object implementation	Array implementation
O(n) Linear	O(1) Constant

A linked list is a dynamic data structure. When implemented using object-oriented techniques, its memory footprint grows and shrinks as data is added and deleted from the structure. Using only as much memory as needed is the most efficient way of implementing a linked list.

However, a linked list could also be implemented using an array. In this case, the dynamic structure is created upon a static data structure and the memory footprint remains constant. This method is inefficient because the linked list will be reserving more memory than it needs unless it is full.

Time complexity of operations on a linked list

Best case	Average case	Worst case
O(1) Constant	O(n) Linear	O(n) Linear

If the order of items is important, you can find the correct position to add or delete a node using a linear search. At best, a new node becomes the first node O(1), or it is the first to be deleted: O(1). Typically, this will not be the case, resulting in a linear complexity when finding the correct position to add or delete a node: O(n).

If the order of the items in a linked list is not important, adding a new item will always have a time complexity: O(1). In this situation, a pointer to the last item would be used to prevent having to follow the pointers from node to node to find the position of the last item in the structure.

Queue

A queue is a linear data structure. Items are "enqueued" at the back of the queue and "dequeued" from the front of the queue. It is also possible to "peek" at the front item without deleting the item.

Imagine a queue at a checkout. The person at the front of the queue is served first, and people join the back of the queue. This strict process can also allow for people to jump the queue — when implemented in computer science, this is known as a **priority queue**. In special circumstances, new items can join the front or the back of the queue.

A queue is known as a first-in, first-out or **FIFO** structure.

A queue has a "back pointer" that always points to the last item in the queue, sometimes referred to as a tail pointer. A queue also has a "front pointer" that always points to the first item in the queue, sometimes referred to as a head pointer.

An attempt to enqueue an item to an already-full queue is called a **queue overflow**, while trying to dequeue an item from an empty queue is called a **queue underflow**. Both should be considered before proceeding to enqueue or dequeue the item in question.

Queues can be implemented using an array or object-oriented technique.

Visualising the implementation of a queue using objects

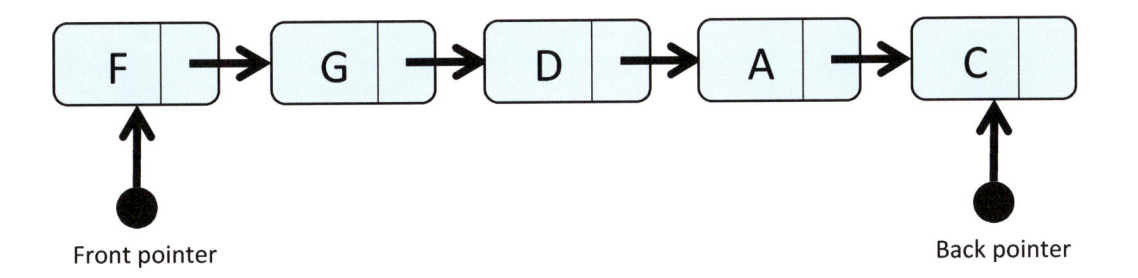

F → G → D → A → C

Front pointer (points to F)
Back pointer (points to C)

Visualising the implementation of a queue using an array

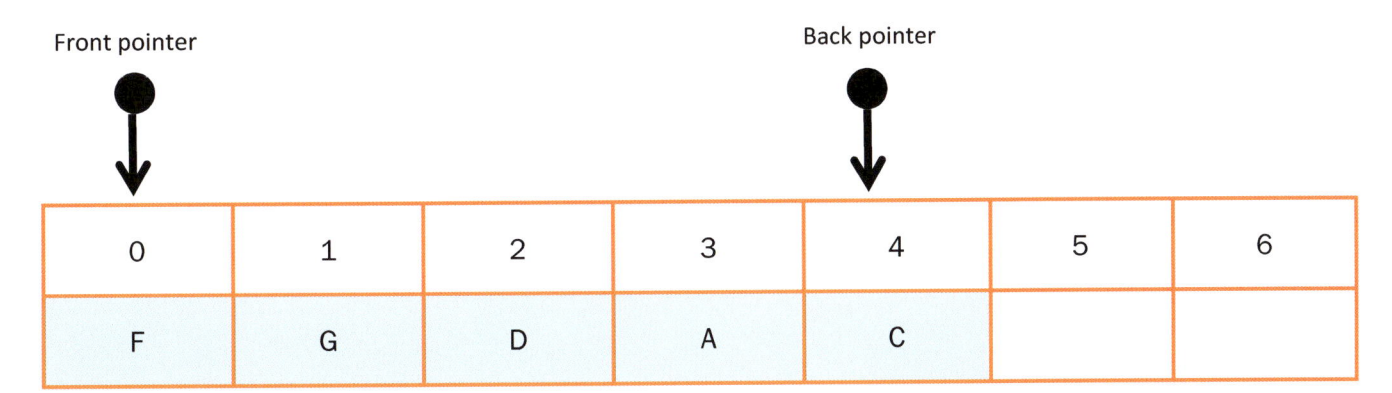

Front pointer → index 0
Back pointer → index 4

0	1	2	3	4	5	6
F	G	D	A	C		

Essential algorithms for A level Computer Science

Circular queues

A problem arises when implementing a queue using an array. Since both the back and front pointers are moving in the same direction as items are added and removed from the queue, the array will quickly run out of free space. The solution is to cycle the back pointer to the front of the array when it reaches the end. This implementation is called a circular queue and is not necessary when implementing a queue using object-oriented techniques.

An array with a circular queue is ideal if you want to restrict the number of items and have a known memory footprint. It is particularly useful in game design, where the number of sprites on the screen will affect the framerate. By only spawning sprites up to the limit of the queue, a stable framerate can be achieved.

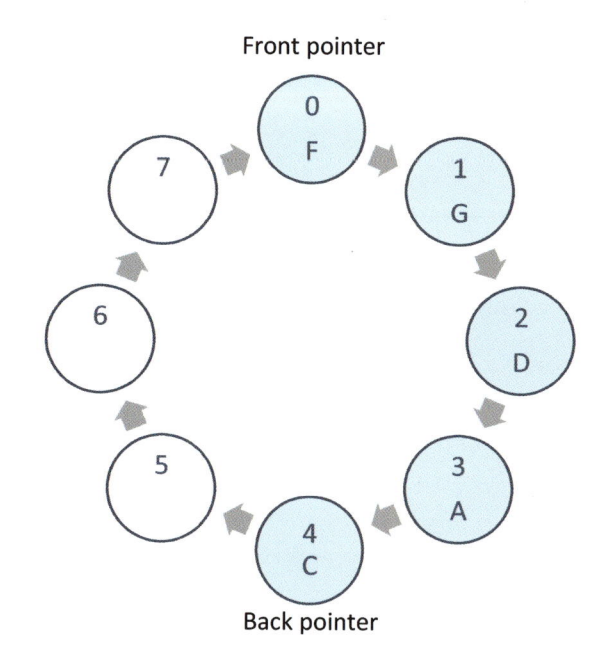

Applications of a queue

Queues are used for process scheduling, transferring data between processors and printer spooling. They are also used to perform breadth-first searches on graph data structures.

Operations on a queue

Typical operations that can be performed on a queue include:

- Enqueue: adding an item to the back of the queue
- Dequeue: removing an item from the front of the queue
- Peek: returning the value from the front of the queue without removing it

Craig'n'Dave videos

https://www.craigndave.org/algorithm-queue

80

Enqueuing an item in simple-structured English

1. Check for queue overflow. Output an error if no free memory is available.
2. Create a new node and insert data into it.
3. The back pointer is set to point to the new node.
4. If this is the first node in the list, the front pointer is set to point to the new node.

Enqueuing an item onto a queue illustrated

If illustrations help you remember, this is how you can picture enqueuing an item:

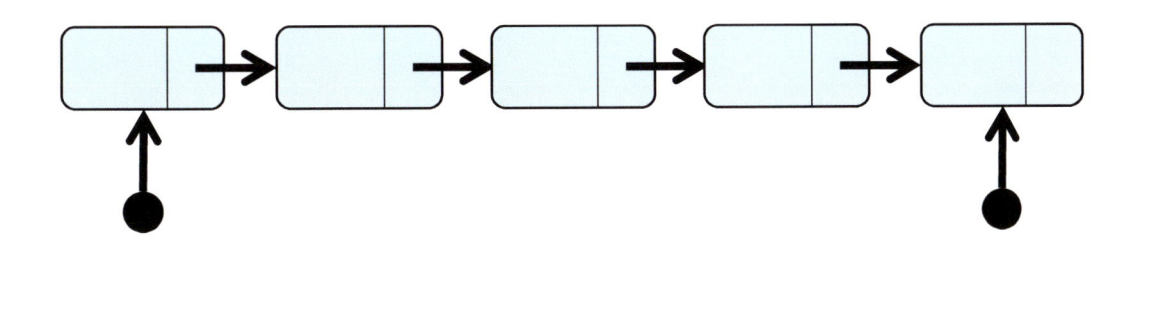

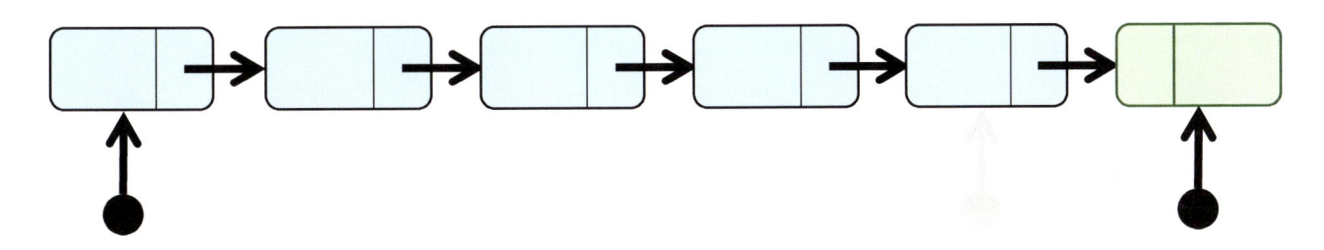

Pseudocode for enqueuing an item

```
If not memoryfull Then
        new_node = New Node
        If back_pointer = Null Then
                front_pointer = new_node
        Else
                Previous_back_node.pointer = new_node
        End If
        Back_pointer = new_node
End If
```

Dequeuing an item in simple-structured English

1. Check for queue underflow. Output an error if the front pointer does not point to a node.
2. Output the node pointed to by the front pointer.
3. Set the front pointer to the previous item.

Dequeuing an item illustrated

If illustrations help you remember, this is how you can picture dequeuing an item:

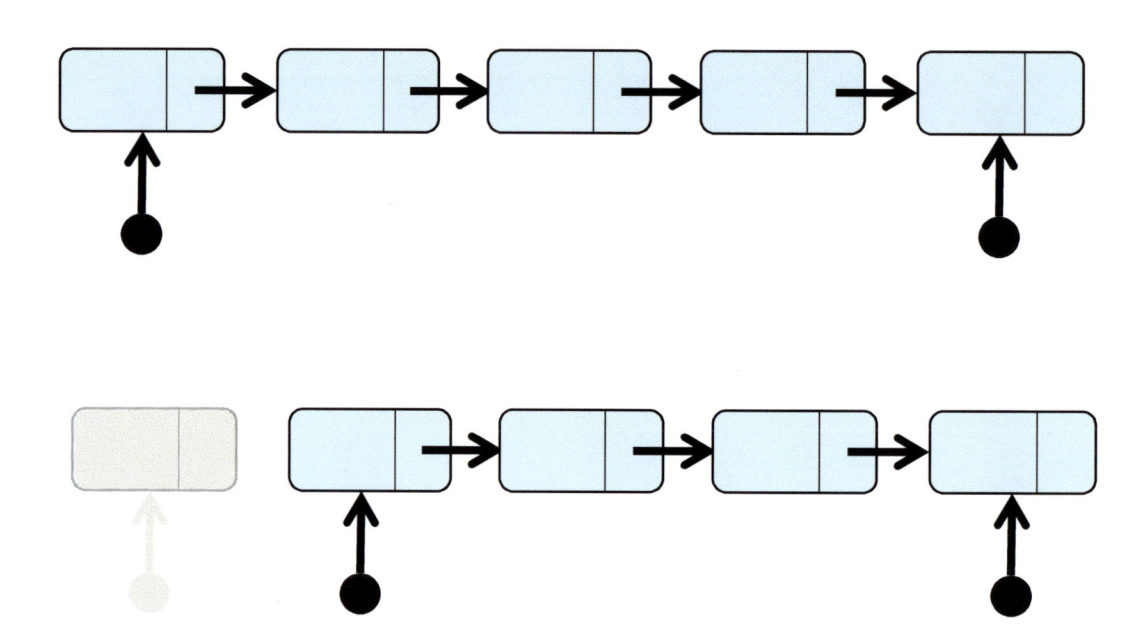

Pseudocode for dequeuing an item

```
If front_pointer != Null Then
      Output front_pointer.data
      front_pointer = front_pointer.pointer
      If front_pointer = Null Then back_pointer = Null
End If
```

Peeking an item from a queue in simple-structured English

1. Output an error if the front pointer does not point to a node.
2. Output the node pointed to by the front pointer.

Pseudocode for peeking an item from a queue

```
If front_apointer != Null Then
      Output front_pointer.data
End If
```

Queue coded in Python

```python
class queue:

    class node:
        data = None
        pointer = None

    front_pointer = None
    back_pointer = None

    def enqueue(self,item):
        #Check queue overflow
        try:
            #Push the item
            new_node = queue.node()
            new_node.data = item
            #Empty queue
            if self.back_pointer == None:
                self.front_pointer = new_node
            else:
                self.back_pointer.pointer = new_node
            self.back_pointer = new_node
            return True
        except:
            return False

    def dequeue(self):
        #Check queue underflow
        if self.front_pointer != None:
            #Pop the item
            popped = self.front_pointer.data
            self.front_pointer = self.front_pointer.pointer
            #When the last item is popped reset the pointers
            if self.front_pointer == None:
                self.back_pointer = None
            return popped
        else:
            return None

    def peek(self):
        #Check stack underflow
        if self.front_pointer != None:
            #Peek the item
            return self.front_pointer.data
        else:
            return None
```

Essential algorithms for A level Computer Science

Enqueuing items to a queue object in Python

```python
items = ["Florida","Georgia","Delaware","Alabama","California"]
q = queue()
for index in range(0,len(items)):
    q.enqueue(items[index])
```

Dequeuing items from a queue object in Python

```python
print(q.dequeue())
```

Peeking a queue object in Python

```python
print(q.peek())
```

Queue coded in Visual Basic Console

```vb
Module Module1
    Public Class queue

        Private Class node
            Public data As String
            Public pointer As node
        End Class

        Private front_pointer As node
        Private back_pointer As node

        Function enqueue(item As String)
            'Check memory overflow
            Try
                'Push the item
                Dim new_node As New node
                new_node.data = item
                'Empty queue
                If IsNothing(back_pointer) Then
                    front_pointer = new_node
                Else
                    back_pointer.pointer = new_node
                End If
                back_pointer = new_node
                Return True
            Catch
                Return False
            End Try
        End Function

        Function dequeue()
            'Check queue underflow
            If Not IsNothing(front_pointer) Then
                'Dequeue the item
```

```vbnet
            Dim popped As String = front_pointer.data
            front_pointer = front_pointer.pointer
            'When the last item is dequeued reset the pointers
            If IsNothing(front_pointer) Then
                back_pointer = Nothing
            End If
            Return popped
        Else
            Return Nothing
        End If
    End Function

    Function peek()
        'Check queue underflow
        If Not IsNothing(front_pointer) Then
            'Peek the item
            Return front_pointer.data
        Else
            Return Nothing
        End If
    End Function
  End Class
End Module
Enqueuing items to a queue object in Visual Basic Console
Dim items() As String = {"Florida", "Georgia", "Delaware", "Alabama", "California"}
Dim q As New queue
For index = 0 To items.Length - 1
q.enqueue(items(index))
Next
```

Dequeuing items from a queue object in Visual Basic Console

```vbnet
Console.WriteLine(q.dequeue)
```

Peeking a queue object in Visual Basic Console

```vbnet
Console.WriteLine(q.peek)
```

Efficiency of a queue

Space complexity of a queue

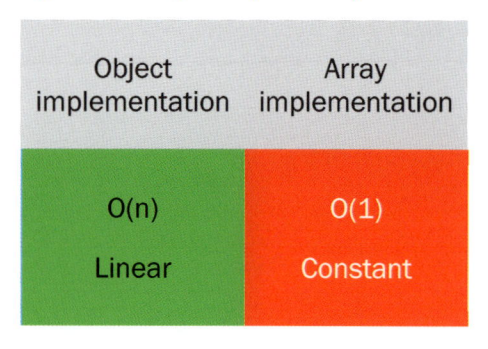

Object implementation	Array implementation
O(n) Linear	O(1) Constant

A queue is a dynamic data structure. When implemented using object-oriented techniques, its memory footprint grows and shrinks as data is enqueued and dequeued from the structure. Using only as much memory as needed is the most efficient way of implementing a queue.

However, a queue could also be implemented using an array. In this case, the dynamic structure has been created upon a static data structure, so the memory footprint remains constant. This method is inefficient because the queue will be reserving more memory than it needs unless it is full.

Time complexity of operations on a queue

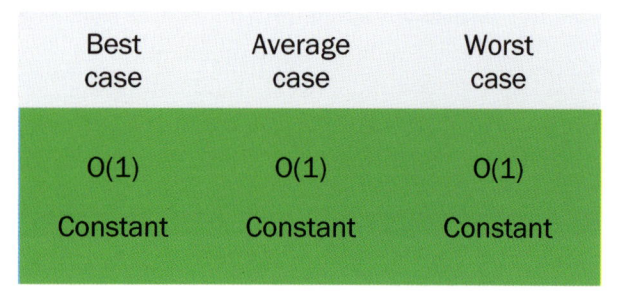

Best case	Average case	Worst case
O(1) Constant	O(1) Constant	O(1) Constant

Items are enqueued at the back of the queue and dequeued from the front. Therefore, the time complexity of all operations on a queue is constant: O(1).

Stack

A stack is an essential data structure for the operation of a computer. Items are "pushed" onto the top of the stack when added and "popped" off the top of the stack when deleted. It is also possible to "peek" at the top item without deleting it.

Imagine a stack of coins. A coin can be added or removed from the top but not the middle. The only way of accessing items in the stack is from the top.

A stack is known as a last-in, first-out or **LIFO** structure. The last item pushed must be the first item popped.

A stack has a "stack pointer" that always points to the node at the top of the stack.

An attempt to push an item to an already-full stack is called a **stack overflow,** while attempting to pop an item from an empty stack is called a **stack underflow.** Both should be considered before proceeding to push or pop the item in question.

A stack is often implemented using an array but can also be created using object-oriented techniques.

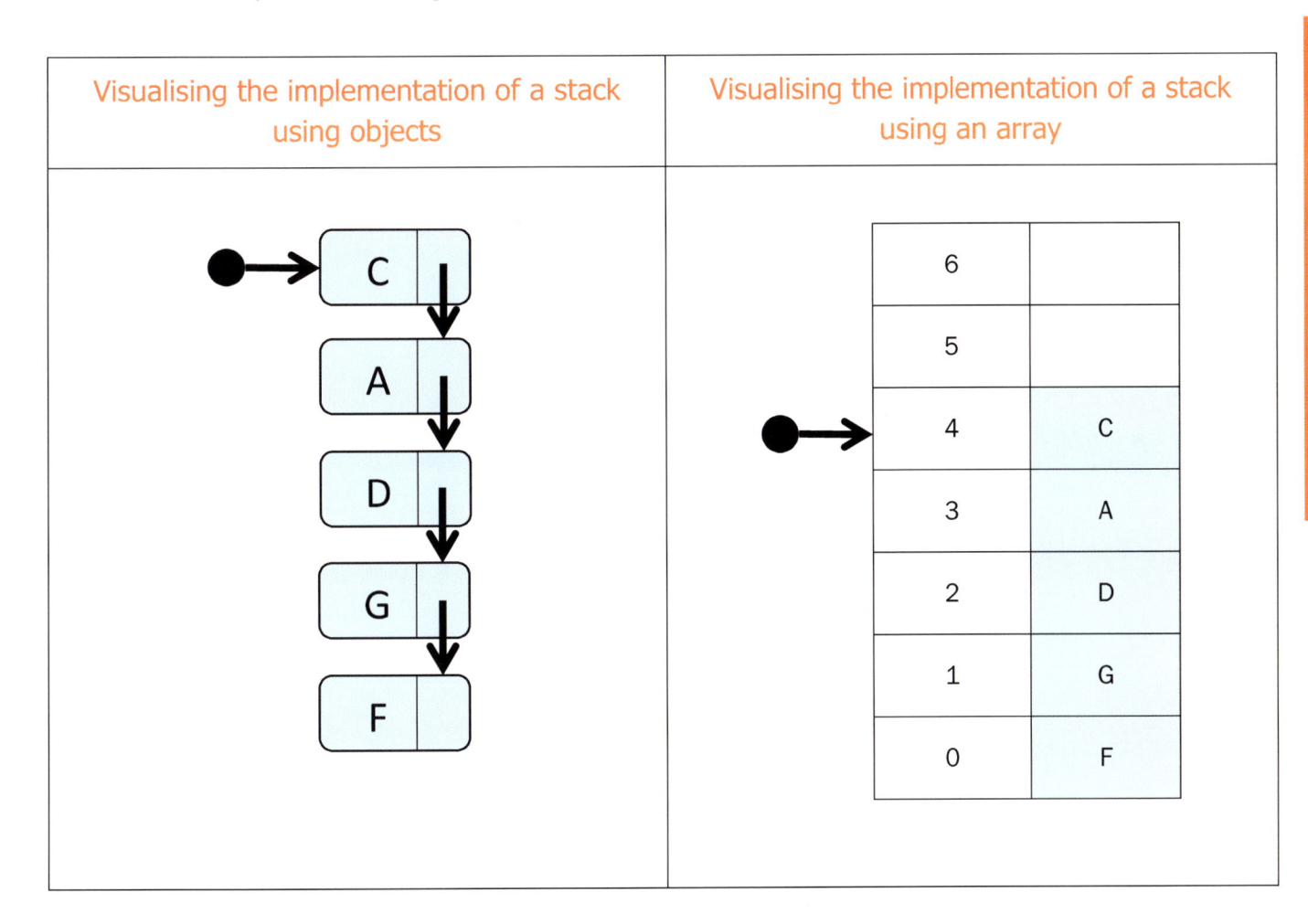

Visualising the implementation of a stack using objects	Visualising the implementation of a stack using an array
C → A → D → G → F	6 — 5 — 4 C ← 3 A 2 D 1 G 0 F

Applications of a stack

Stacks are used by processors to keep track of program flow. When a procedure or function (subroutine) is called, it changes the value of the program counter to the first instruction of the subroutine. When the subroutine ends, the processor must return the program counter to its value from before the subroutine was called. We can achieve this using a stack, allowing subroutine calls to be nested. Local variables are also held on the stack, which is why their value is lost when a subroutine ends — because they are popped off the stack. Interrupts can also be handled with a stack in the same way.

Stacks are used to perform depth-first searches on graph data structures, undo operations when keeping track of user inputs and backtracking algorithms — for example, pathfinding maze solutions. Stacks are also used to evaluate mathematical expressions without brackets, using a shunting yard algorithm and reverse Polish notation.

Operations on a stack

Typical operations that can be performed on a stack include:

- Push: adding an item to the top of the stack
- Pop: removing an item from the top of the stack
- Peek: returning the value from the top of the stack without removing it

Craig'n'Dave videos

https://www.craigndave.org/algorithm-stack

Pushing an item onto a stack in simple-structured English

1. Check for stack overflow. Output an error if no free memory is available.
2. Create a new node and insert data into it.
3. The new node points to the previous node.
4. The stack pointer is set to point to the new node.

Higher order data structures

Pushing an item onto a stack illustrated

If illustrations help you remember, this is how you can picture pushing an item onto a stack:

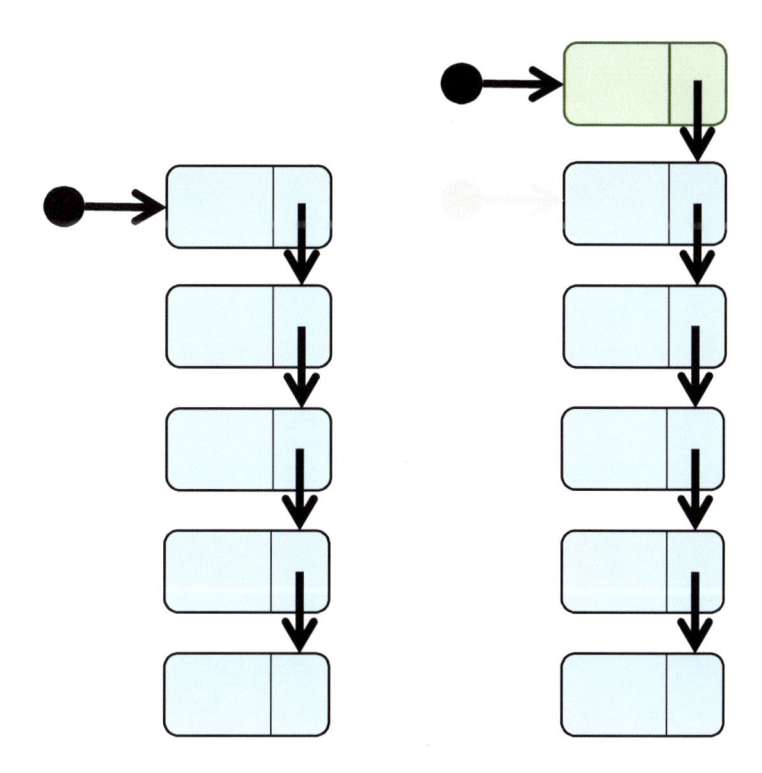

Pseudocode for pushing an item onto a stack

```
If not memoryfull Then
      new_node = New Node
      new_node.pointer = stack_pointer
      stack_pointer = new_node
End If
```

💡 Did you know?

Popping is sometimes called "pulling."

In addition to pushing, popping and peeking items from a stack, a third operation called "rotate" or "roll" can be used to move items around a stack. "A-B-C" on a stack becomes "B-C-A," where the first item has "rolled" to become the last item.

Popping an item from a stack in simple-structured English

1. Check for stack underflow. Output an error if the stack pointer does not point to a node.
2. Output the node pointed to by the stack pointer.
3. Set the stack pointer to the previous item.

Popping an item from a stack illustrated

If illustrations help you remember, this is how you can picture popping an item from a stack:

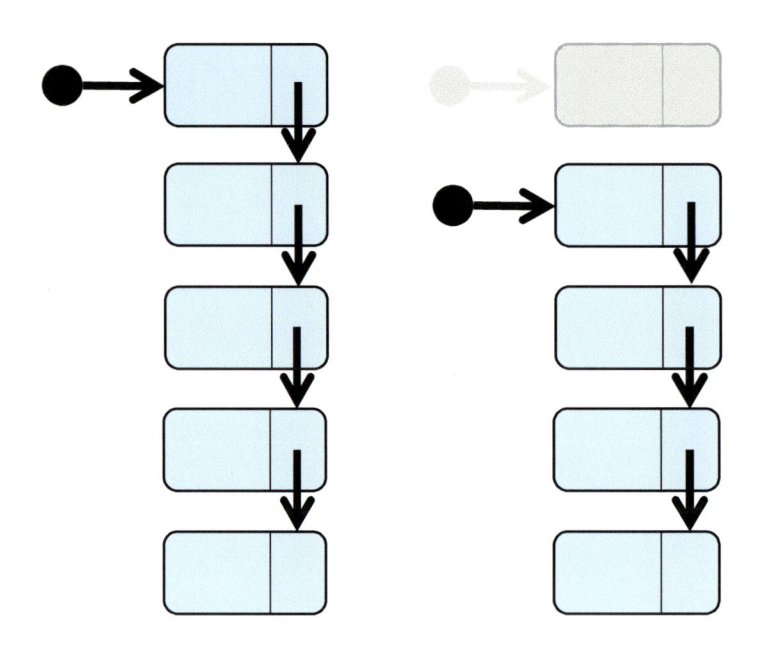

Pseudocode for popping an item from a stack

```
If stack_pointer != Null Then
        Output stack_pointer.data
        stack_pointer = stack_pointer.pointer
End If
```

Peeking an item from a stack in simple-structured English

1. Output an error if the stack pointer does not point to a node.
2. Output the node pointed to by the stack pointer.

Pseudocode for peeking an item from a stack

```
If stack_pointer != Null Then
    Output stack_pointer.data
End If
```

Stack coded in Python

```python
class stack:

    class node:
        data = None
        pointer = None

    stack_pointer = None

    def push(self,item):
        #Check stack overflow
        try:
            #Push the item
            new_node = stack.node()
            new_node.data = item
            new_node.pointer = self.stack_pointer
            self.stack_pointer = new_node
            return True
        except:
            return False

    def pop(self):
        #Check stack underflow
        if self.stack_pointer != None:
            #Pop the item
            popped = self.stack_pointer.data
            self.stack_pointer = self.stack_pointer.pointer
            return popped
        else:
            return None

    def peek(self):
        #Check stack underflow
        if self.stack_pointer != None:
            #Peek the item
```

Essential algorithms for A level Computer Science

```python
            return self.stack_pointer.data
        else:
            return None
```

Pushing items to a stack object in Python

```python
items = ["Florida","Georgia","Delaware","Alabama","California"]
s = stack()
for index in range(0,len(items)):
    s.push(items[index])
```

Popping items from a stack object in Python

```python
print(s.pop())
```

Peeking a stack object in Python

```python
print(s.peek())
```

Stack coded in Visual Basic Console

```vb
Module Module1
    Public Class stack

        Private Class node
            Public data As String
            Public pointer As node
        End Class

        Private stack_pointer As node

        Function push(item As String)
            'Check memory overflow
            Try
                'Push the item
                Dim new_node As New node
                new_node.data = item
                new_node.pointer = stack_pointer
                stack_pointer = new_node
                Return True
            Catch
                Return False
            End Try
        End Function

        Function pop()
            'Check stack underflow
            If Not IsNothing(stack_pointer) Then
                'Pop the item
                Dim popped As String = stack_pointer.data
                stack_pointer = stack_pointer.pointer
                Return popped
```

```vbnet
            Else
                Return Nothing
            End If
        End Function

        Function peek()
            'Check stack underflow
            If Not IsNothing(stack_pointer) Then
                'Peek the item
                Return stack_pointer.data
            Else
                Return Nothing
            End If
        End Function
    End Class

End Module
```

Pushing items to a stack object in Visual Basic Console

```vbnet
Dim items() As String = {"Florida", "Georgia", "Delaware", "Alabama", "California"}
Dim s As New stack
For index = 0 To items.Length - 1
s.push(items(index))
Next
```

Popping items from a stack object in Visual Basic Console

```vbnet
Console.WriteLine(s.pop)
```

Peeking a stack object in Visual Basic Console

```vbnet
Console.WriteLine(s.peek)
```

> ### Did you know?
>
> Other operations on a stack include "duplicate," where the top item is popped and then pushed twice, and "swap" or "exchange," where the top-two items are popped and then pushed back to the stack in the opposite order.
>
> While these additional operations do not feature in the specification, showing examples of them can make great exam questions to test your understanding of how a stack works.

Efficiency of a stack

Space complexity of a stack

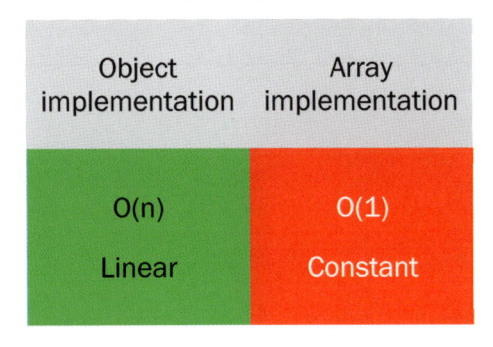

Object implementation	Array implementation
O(n) Linear	O(1) Constant

A stack is a dynamic data structure. When implemented using object-oriented techniques, its memory footprint grows and shrinks as data is pushed onto and popped from the structure. Using only as much memory as needed is the most efficient way of implementing a stack.

However, a stack could also be implemented using an array. In this case, the dynamic structure has been created upon a static data structure, so the memory footprint remains constant. This method is inefficient because the stack will be reserving more memory than it needs unless it is full.

Time complexity of operations on a stack

Best case	Average case	Worst case
O(1) Constant	O(1) Constant	O(1) Constant

Items are always pushed onto and popped from the top of the stack. Therefore, the time complexity of all operations on a stack is constant: O(1).

Did you know?

Stacks are always shown vertically in illustrations, but there is no reason why a stack cannot be visualised horizontally, making it look like a linked list — the difference being how the pointers allow for pushing and popping operations.

In summary

Stack

LIFO – last-in, first-out structure

Items are inserted (pushed) onto and deleted (popped) from the top of the structure

One pointer at the top of the structure

Queue

FIFO – first-in, first-out structure

Items are inserted (enqueued) to the back of the structure.

Items are removed (dequeued) from the front of the structure

Two pointers — one at the back of the structure and one at the front

Graph

Nodes can have more than two child nodes

Many paths to different nodes — loops are permitted between nodes

Any node can be a root node — a starting point for breadth and depth-first searches

Nodes often referred to as vertices; pointers referred to as edges

Used to represent related data

Binary tree

A special case of a graph where nodes can only have up to two child nodes

One path to a node

One root node — the starting point for all operations

Nodes at the end of the structure referred to as leaf nodes

Can be used to implement binary searches (binary search tree) and dictionaries

Linked list

Is the same data structure as a list

May have special implementations enabling it to be doubly linked or circular

SEARCHING ALGORITHMS

Routines that find data within a data structure.

Binary search

Searching algorithms

The binary search is an efficient algorithm for finding an item in a **sorted list**. To perform a binary search, start at the middle item in the list and repeatedly divide the list in half.

Applications of a binary search

Any situation where you need to search for an item in a large, sorted data set.

Craig'n'Dave videos

https://www.craigndave.org/algorithm-binary-search

Binary search in simple-structured English

1. Start at the middle item in the list.
2. If the middle item is the one to be found, the search is complete.
3. If the item to be found is lower than the middle item, discard all items to the right.
4. If the item to be found is higher than the middle item, discard all items to the left.
5. Repeat from step 2 until you have found the item or there are no more items in the list.
6. If the item has been found, output item data. If it has not, output "not found."

Binary search illustrated

If illustrations help you remember, this is how you can picture a binary search:

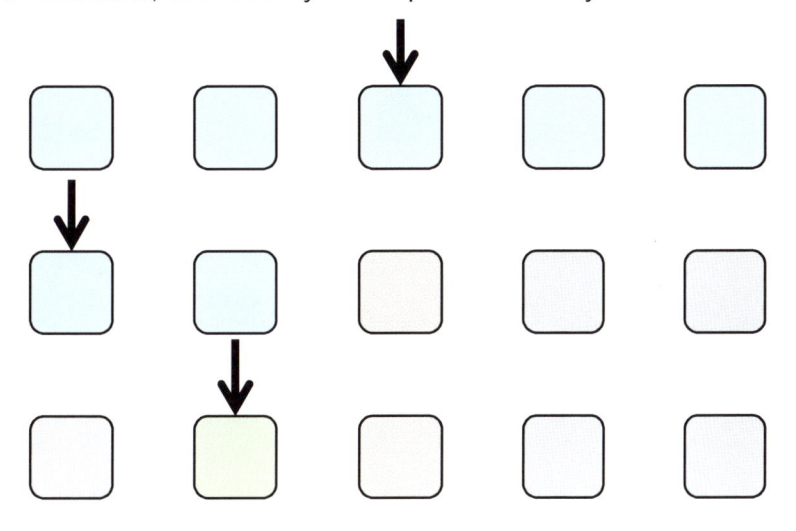

Essential algorithms for A level Computer Science

Stepping through the binary search

Searching for California:

Index:	0	1	2	3	4
Step 1	Calculate the middle as the first index (0) + the last index (4) integer division by 2 = 2: Delaware				
	Alabama	California	**Delaware**	Florida	Georgia
Step 2	Delaware is not the item to be found. California is lower. Discard all items to the right.				
	Alabama	California	Delaware	Florida	Georgia
Step 3	Calculate the middle as the first index (0) + the last index (1) integer division by 2: = 0: Alabama				
	Alabama	California	Delaware	Florida	Georgia
Step 4	Alabama is not the item to be found. California is higher. Discard all items to the left.				
	Alabama	California	Delaware	Florida	Georgia
Step 5	Calculate the middle as the first index (1) + the last index (1 integer division by 2 = 1: California				
	Alabama	**California**	Delaware	Florida	Georgia
	Item found in the list.				

Three comparisons were needed to find the item.

Note how the number of items to be checked is halved after each comparison. This is what makes the binary search so efficient, but it also explains why the items must be in order for the algorithm to work.

Pseudocode for the binary search

```
items = ["Alabama","California","Delaware","Florida","Georgia"]
item_to_find = input("Enter the state to find: ")
found = False
first = 0
last = items.Length -1
While first <= last and found == False
        Midpoint = (first + last) DIV 2
        If items[midpoint] == item_to_find then
                found = True
        Else
                If items[midpoint] < item_to_find then
                        first = midpoint + 1
                Else
                        last = midpoint - 1
                End If
        End If
End while
If found == True then
        Print "Item found at position ",midpoint
Else
        Print "Item not found"
End If
```

Did you know?

These examples illustrate a binary search using an array or list. A binary search can also be performed on a binary tree. In this situation, it is known as a binary search tree.

Binary search coded in Python

The following code checks if the letter "D" is located in a sorted list.

```python
items = ["Alabama","California","Delaware","Florida","Georgia"]
item_to_find = input("Enter the state to find: ")
found = False
first = 0
last = len(items) -1
while first <= last and found == False:
    midpoint = (first + last) // 2
    if items[midpoint] == item_to_find:
        found = True
    else:
        if items[midpoint] < item_to_find:
            first = midpoint + 1
        else:
            last = midpoint - 1
if found == True:
    print("Item found at position",midpoint)
else:
    print("Item not found")
```

Did you know?

As the binary search requires a calculation of the mid-point, the algorithm can fail in certain situations. "Midpoint = (first + last) DIV 2" can result in an arithmetic overflow in situations where the number of indices exceeds the maximum value for an integer. The Java programming language had this bug in a library providing a binary search function for more than nine years.

Binary search coded in Visual Basic Console

```vb
Module Module1
    Sub Main()
        Dim items() As String = {"Florida", "California", "Delaware", "Alabama", "Georgia"}
        Dim item_to_find As String
        Dim found As Boolean = False
        Dim first As Integer = 0
        Dim midpoint As Integer = 0
        Dim last As Integer = items.Count - 1
        Console.WriteLine("Enter the state to find: ")
        item_to_find = Console.ReadLine
        While first <= last And found = False
            midpoint = (first + last) \ 2
            If items(midpoint) = item_to_find Then
                found = True
            Else
                If items(midpoint) < item_to_find Then
                    first = midpoint + 1
                Else
                    last = midpoint - 1
                End If
            End If
        End While
        If found = True Then
            Console.WriteLine("Item found at position " & midpoint)
        Else
            Console.WriteLine("Item not found")
        End If
        Console.ReadLine()
    End Sub
End Module
```

Did you know?

There are many different types of binary search, including uniform, exponential, interpolation, fractional cascading, noisy and quantum. Thankfully, you only need to know about the classic binary search for examinations.

Efficiency of the binary search

A binary search can be performed on an array or binary tree data structure.

Time complexity

	Best case	Average case	Worst case
Binarcy search array	O(1) Constant	O(log n) Logarithmic	O(log n) Logarithmic
Binary search tree	O(1) Constant	O(log n) Logarithmic	O(n) Linear

A binary search will usually be more efficient than a linear search, although it does require the data set to be sorted if a binary tree is not used as the underlying data structure.

In the best case, the item to be found is either in the middle position of an array or at the root node of a binary tree. In this special case, the algorithm has a time complexity of O(1) since the item to be found will always be the first item checked. However, this is not usually the case.

In most cases, the time it takes to find an item increases with the size of the data set. However, because half of the items can be discarded at a time, the algorithm is usually logarithmic: O(log n).

If a binary tree is used to store the data, it is possible that an unbalanced tree could be created:

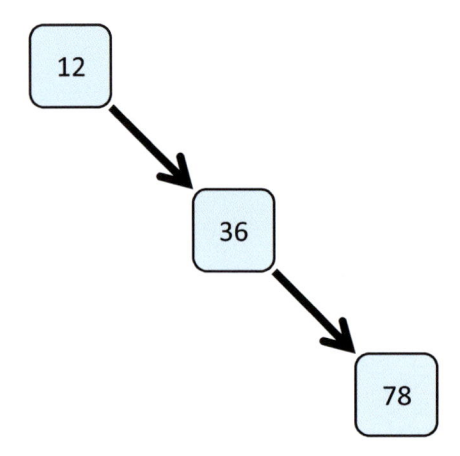

```
12
  ↓
   36
     ↓
      78
```

In this worst case, to find the number 78 would require checking all the items in the data set, reducing the time complexity of the algorithm to O(n). This does not usually happen, and the goal is to use a binary tree only when the data is likely to create a more balanced structure. Alternatively, you may use it to avoid sorting the data before applying the binary search.

Hash table search

The goal with a hash table is to immediately find an item in a sorted or unsorted list without the need to compare other items in the data set. It is how programming languages implement a dictionary data structure. A **hashing function** is used to calculate the position of an item in a hash table.

Applications of a hash table search

Hash tables are used in situations where items in a large data set need to be found quickly.

Craig'n'Dave videos

https://www.craigndave.org/algorithm-hash-table-search

How hash tables work

Creating a hash table

A hashing function is applied to an item to determine a hash value — the position of the item in a hash table. There are many different hashing functions in use today. A simple example might be to add up the ASCII values of all the characters in a string and calculate the modulus of that value by the size of the hash table.

E.g., assuming a table size of 10:

Florida: F = 70, l = 108, o = 111, r = 114, i = 105, d = 100, a = 97
70+108+111+114+105+100+97 = 705
705 mod 10 = 5
The position of Florida in the table is 5.

A hash table needs to be at least large enough to store all the data items but is usually significantly larger to minimise the algorithm returning the same value for more than one item, known as a **collision**, e.g.:

Delaware: D = 68, e = 101, l = 108, a = 97, w = 119, a = 97, r = 114, e =101
68+101+108+97+119+97+114+101 = 805
805 mod 10 = 5
The position of Delaware in the table is 5.

Since two items of data cannot occupy the same position in the hash table, a collision has occurred.

Essential algorithms for A level Computer Science

Properties of good hashing functions

A good hashing function should:

1. Be calculated quickly.
2. Result in as few collisions as possible.
3. Use as little memory as possible.

Resolving collisions

There are many strategies to resolve collisions generated from hashing functions. A simple solution is to repeatedly check the next available space in the hash table until an empty position is found and store the item in that location. This is known as open addressing. To find the item later, the hashing function delivers the start position from which a linear search can then be applied until the item is found.

This is known as linear probing:

1	2	3	4	5	6	7	8	9	10
Alabama	Georgia			Florida	Delaware	California			

In this example, we can see that Delaware has a hash value of 5, but that is occupied by Florida. Delaware is therefore placed at 6, the next available position. California has a hash value of 6 but cannot occupy its intended position, so it must be stored at the next available position, 7.

A disadvantage of linear probing in this way is that it will prevent other items being stored at their correct location in the hash table. It also results in what is known as clustering — several positions being filled around common collision values.

Notice that with a table size of 10, two collisions occur. With a table size of 5, three collisions occur, resulting in a less efficient algorithm but a reduced memory footprint. If the table size is increased to 11, no collisions occur. With hashing algorithms, there is often a trade-off between the efficiency of the algorithm and the size of the hash table.

A potential solution to clustering is to skip several positions before storing the item, resulting in more even distribution throughout the table. A simple approach would be to skip to every third item. A variation of this, known as quadratic probing, increases the number of items skipped with each jump — e.g., 1, 4, 9, 16.

It may also be necessary to increase the size of the hash table in the future and recalculate the new position of all the items in the table.

The process of finding an alternative position for items in the hash table is known as **rehashing**.

An alternative method of handling collisions is to use a two-dimensional hash table. It is then possible for more than one item to be placed at the same position. This is known as chaining:

	1	2	3	4	5	6	7	8	9	10
0	Alabama	Georgia			Florida	California				
1					Delaware					

In this example, we can see that both Florida and Delaware can occupy the same position but a different element of the 2D array.

Another possibility would be to use a second table for all collisions, known as an overflow table:

1	2	3	4	5	6	7	8	9	10
Alabama	Georgia			Florida	California				

0	1	2	3	4	5	6	7	8	9
Delaware									

Hash table search in simple-structured English

1. Calculate the position of the item in the hash table using a hashing function.
2. Check if the item at that position is the item to be found.
3. If it is not, move to the next item.
4. Repeat from step 2 until the item is found or there are no more items in the hash table.
5. If the item has been found, output item data. If it has not, output "not found."

Essential algorithms for A level Computer Science

Hash table search illustrated

If illustrations help you remember, this is how you can picture a hash search:

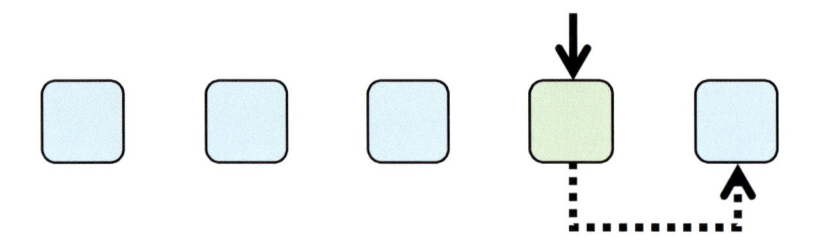

Stepping through the hash table search

Searching for California:

Index:	1	2	3	4	5	6	7	8	9	10
Step 1	Calculate the hash value for California: C = 67, a = 97, l = 108, l = 105, f = 102, o =111, r =114, n = 110, l = 105, a = 97 67+97+108+105+102+111+114+110+105+97 = 1016 1016 mod 10 = 6. Compare California to Delaware. Delaware is not the item to be found. Move to the next item in the hash table.									
	Alabama	Georgia				Florida	Delaware	California		
Step 2	Compare California to California. Item found.									
	Alabama	Georgia				Florida	Delaware	California		

Two comparisons were needed to find the item.

Pseudocode for the hash table search

```
items = ["Florida","Georgia","Delaware","Alabama","California"]
hash_table = create_hash_table(items)
item_to_find = input("Enter the state to find: ")
h = calculate_hash(item_to_find)
If hash_table(h) != "":
      If hash_table(h) == item_to_find:
            Found = True
      Else
            Do While h < hash_table.Length and not found:
                  If hash_table(h) != item_to_find:
                        h = h + 1
                  Else
                        found = True
                  End If
            End While
      End If
End If
If found == True then
      Print "Item found at position ",index
Else
      Print "Item not found"
End If
```

Did you know?

The efficiency of a hash table search is reliant on the suitability of the hashing function. If the data set is known in advance and does not change, it is possible to construct a perfect hash function that guarantees constant time complexity without any collisions.

Essential algorithms for A level Computer Science

Hash table search coded in Python

```python
def calculate_hash(item, table_size):
    #Simple hashing algorithm adds ascii values of characters
    total = 0
    for character in range(len(item)):
        total = total + ord(item[character])
    return total % table_size

def create_hash_table(items, table_size):
    #Reserve memory for hashing table
    hash_table = []
    for counter in range(table_size):
            hash_table.append("")
    #Place data into hashing table
    for index in range(len(items)):
        h = calculate_hash(items[index],table_size)
        if hash_table[h] != "":
            print("Collision inserting",items[index],"at",h)
            #On collision insert in next available space
            while hash_table[h] != "":
                h = h + 1
        hash_table[h] = items[index]
        print("Inserted",items[index],"at position",h)
    return hash_table

def search_hash_table(item_to_find, hash_table):
    found = False
    h = calculate_hash(item_to_find, len(hash_table))
    #Attempt to find item at hash value
    if hash_table[h] != "":
        if hash_table[h] == item_to_find:
            found = True
        else:
            #Degrade to linear search for collisions
            while h<len(hash_table) and not found:
                if hash_table[h] != item_to_find:
                    h = h + 1
                else:
                    found = True
    if found:
        print ("Item found at position",h)
    else:
        print("Item not found")

#Main algorithm starts here
items = ["Florida","Georgia","Delaware","Alabama","California"]
#The larger the table the fewer collisions
table_size = 10
```

```vb
hash_table = create_hash_table(items, table_size)
item_to_find = input("Enter the state to find: ")
search_hash_table(item_to_find, hash_table)
```

Hash table search coded in Visual Basic Console

```vb
Module Module1
    Function calculate_hash(item As String, table_size As Integer)
        'Simple hashing algorithm adds ascii values of characters
        Dim total As Integer = 0
        For character = 1 To Len(item)
            total = total + Asc(Mid(item, character, 1))
        Next
        Return total Mod table_size
    End Function

    Function create_hash_table(items As Array, table_size As Integer)
        'Reserve memory for hashing table
        Dim hash_table(table_size) As String
        Dim h As Integer
        'Place data in hashing table
        For index = 0 To items.Length - 1
            h = calculate_hash(items(index), table_size)
            If hash_table(h) <> "" Then
                Console.WriteLine("Collision inserting " & items(index) & " at " & h)
                'On collision insert in next available space
                Do While hash_table(h) <> ""
                    h = h + 1
                Loop
            End If
            hash_table(h) = items(index)
            Console.WriteLine("Inserted " & items(index) & " at position " & h)
        Next
        Return hash_table
    End Function

    Sub search_hash_table(item_to_find As String, hash_table As Array)
        Dim found As Boolean = False
        Dim h As Integer
        h = calculate_hash(item_to_find, (hash_table.Length - 1))
        'Attempt to find item at hash value
        If hash_table(h) <> "" Then
            If hash_table(h) = item_to_find Then
                found = True
            Else
                'Degrade to linear search for collisions
                Do While h < hash_table.Length And Not found
                    If hash_table(h) <> item_to_find Then
                        h = h + 1
```

```vb
                    Else
                        found = True
                    End If
                Loop
            End If
        End If
        If found Then
            Console.WriteLine("Item found at position " & h)
        Else
            Console.WriteLine("Item not found")
        End If
    End Sub

    'Main algorithm starts here
    Sub Main()
        Dim items() As String = {"Florida", "Georgia", "Delaware", "Alabama", "California"}
        'The larger the table the fewer collisions
        Dim table_size As Integer = 10
        Dim hash_table(table_size) As String
        Dim item_to_find As String
        hash_table = create_hash_table(items, table_size)
        Console.Write("Enter the state to find: ")
        item_to_find = Console.ReadLine
        search_hash_table(item_to_find, hash_table)
        Console.ReadLine()
    End Sub
End Module
```

Did you know?

Hashing functions calculate the position of an item in a hashing table. Items will have a key field that can be used to uniquely identify an item from all the others. Examples include barcodes, ISBN numbers, number plates and NHS numbers. The hashing algorithm is applied to this field.

Hash searching can be used on a hash table stored in memory but is often used with large data sets and, therefore, more commonly used on files. Since it is necessary to move directly to the item to be found and not search through the other items first, a hash search can only be performed on a hard disk, solid-state drive or RAM.

Efficiency of the hash table search

Time complexity		
Best case	Average case	Worst case
O(1) Constant	O(1) Constant	O(n) Linear

The hash table search is usually the most efficient of all the searching algorithms, out-performing a linear search and binary search on average. It achieves this by finding the position of an item immediately using a hashing function, resulting in a constant time complexity of O(1) in both best and average cases.

However, if the item cannot be found immediately because of a collision, a variation of a linear search known as linear probing must be used instead. This results in a time complexity of O(n) since each item must be checked in turn until either the item is found or the end of the table is reached.

With hash searching, it is important to have an efficient hashing function that will calculate quickly but also produce as few collisions as possible. This is often achieved by using a larger hash table than is needed to store the data, increasing the number of unique positions and reducing the number of possible collisions.

Did you know?

It is also a good idea to swap data items where collisions occur, so the more frequently searched item is the one stored in the location determined by the hashing function. This approach is known as "Robin Hood hashing" — steal from the rich to give to the poor!

Essential algorithms for A level Computer Science

Linear search

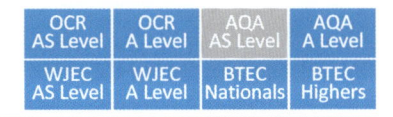

The linear search finds an item in a sorted or unsorted list. To perform a linear search, start at the first item in the list and check each item one by one. Think about searching for a card in a shuffled deck, starting with the top card and checking each one until you find the card you want.

Applications of a linear search

The linear search is ideal for finding items in small data sets and performing searches with unordered data such as settings files. It is the easiest searching algorithm to implement but usually the most inefficient.

Craig'n'Dave videos

https://www.craigndave.org/algorithms-linear-search

Linear search in simple-structured English

1. Start at the first item in the list.
2. If the item in the list is the one to be found, the search is complete.
3. If it is not, move to the next item.
4. Repeat from step 2 until the item is found or there are no more items in the list.
5. If the item has been found, output item data. If it has not, output "not found."

Linear search illustrated

If illustrations help you remember, this is how you can picture a linear search:

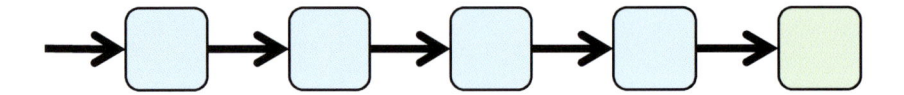

112

Stepping through the linear search

Searching for California:

Index:	0	1	2	3	4
Step 1	Start at the first item in the list. Compare California to Florida. Florida is not the item to be found. Move to the next item in the list.					
	Florida	Georgia	Delaware	Alabama	California
Step 2	Compare California to Georgia. Georgia is not the item to be found. Move to the next item in the list.				
	Florida	**Georgia**	Delaware	Alabama	California
Step 3	Compare California to Delaware. Delaware is not the item to be found. Move to the next item in the list.				
	Florida	Georgia	**Delaware**	Alabama	California
Step 4	Compare California to Alabama. Alabama is not the item to be found. Move to the next item in the list.				
	Florida	Georgia	Delaware	**Alabama**	California
Step 5	Compare California to California. Item found.				
	Florida	Georgia	Delaware	Alabama	**California**

Five comparisons were needed to find the item.

Essential algorithms for A level Computer Science

Pseudocode for the linear search

```
items = ["Florida","Georgia","Delaware","Alabama","California"]
item_to_find = input("Enter the state to find: ")
index = 0
found = False
While found == False and index < items.Length
        If items[index] == item_to_find then
                found = True
        Else
                index = index + 1
        End If
End while
If found == True then
        Print "Item found at position ",index
Else
        Print "Item not found"
End If
```

Linear search coded in Python

```python
items = ["Florida","Georgia","Delaware","Alabama","California"]
item_to_find = input("Enter the state to find: ")
index = 0
found = False
while found == False and index < len(items):
    if items[index] == item_to_find:
        found = True
    else:
        index = index + 1
if found == True:
    print ("Item found at position",index)
else:
    print ("Item not found")
```

Linear search coded in Visual Basic Console

```vb
Module Module1
    Sub Main()
        Dim items() As String = {"Florida", "California", "Delaware", "Alabama", "Georgia"}
        Dim item_to_find As String
        Dim index As Integer = 0
        Dim found As Boolean = False
        Console.WriteLine("Enter the state to find: ")
        item_to_find = Console.ReadLine
        Do While found = False And index < items.Count
            If items(index) = item_to_find Then
                found = True
            Else
                index = index + 1
            End If
        Loop
        If found = True Then
            Console.WriteLine("Item found at position " & index)
        Else
            Console.WriteLine("Item not found")
        End If
        Console.ReadLine()
    End Sub
End Module
```

Did you know?

Due to how quickly modern processors can execute simple instructions and the fact that data does not need to be sorted for the linear search to work, it is a practical solution for any data set that is likely to contain up to a hundred items.

Beyond this, it would be better to use an alternative algorithm. If certain data items are likely to be searched for more frequently, it would be better to place them towards the beginning of the list to maximise the efficiency of the algorithm.

When programming a linear search, use a "while" statement if only one occurrence of an item needs to be found and a "for" statement if all occurrences need to be found.

Efficiency of the linear search

	Time complexity	
Best case	Average case	Worst case
O(1) Constant	O(n) Linear	O(n) Linear

A linear search is only efficient on smaller or unsorted data sets.

In the best case, the item to be found is the first on the list. In this situation, the linear search performs as well as a binary search when the first item is in the middle of the list: O(1).

That means the linear search can perform better than a binary search on very small lists.

In the worst case, the item to be found is last on the list or not in the list at all, so all the items need to be checked: O(n). Typically, the item to be found will be somewhere in the data set and, as the data set grows, more searching must be performed. Therefore, the algorithm has a complexity of O(n).

Did you know?

Linear searches can also be performed on serial files. If you are asked to perform a linear search on a file, don't forget to include a line of pseudocode to open the file before the algorithm and to close the file afterwards. That may be awarded a mark.

In summary

Binary search	Hash table search	Linear search
Items must be in order for the algorithm to work	Items are not stored in any useful order	Items do not need to be stored in order
Start at the middle item	Use a hashing function on the key	Start at the first item
Halve the set of items to search after each comparison until the item is found or there are no more items to check	Hashing function delivers the location of the item to be found unless there is a collision or it doesn't exist	Search each item in sequence until the item is found or there are no more items to check
Log_2N+1 comparisons are needed	Usually 1 comparison is needed, <N at worst	N comparisons are needed
Can be implemented using an array or binary tree	An implementation of a dictionary	Can be implemented using an array or linked list
New items must be added in the correct place to maintain the order of the items — can be slow	New items can be added with the hashing function determining the location — usually quick	New items are added at the end — quick
Suitable for a large number of items	Suitable for a large number of items	Suitable for a small number of items

SORTING ALGORITHMS

Routines that organise data in fundamental data structures.

Bubble Sort

The bubble sort orders an unordered list of items by comparing each item with the next one and swapping them if they are out of order. The algorithm is finished when no swaps are made. It effectively "bubbles up" the largest (or smallest) item to the end of the list.

Applications of a bubble sort

The bubble sort is the most inefficient of the sorting algorithms but is very easy to implement, so it is a popular choice for very small data sets. It is ideal for situations where you want a simple, easy-to-program sorting algorithm.

Craig'n'Dave video

https://www.craigndave.org/algorithm-bubble-sort

Bubble sort in simple-structured English

1. Start at the first item in the list.
2. Compare the current item with the next one.
3. If the two items are in the wrong position, swap them.
4. Move to the next item in the list.
5. Repeat from step 2 until all the unsorted items have been compared.
6. If any items were swapped, repeat from step 1. Otherwise, the algorithm is complete.

Bubble sort illustrated

If illustrations help you remember, this is how you can picture a bubble sort:

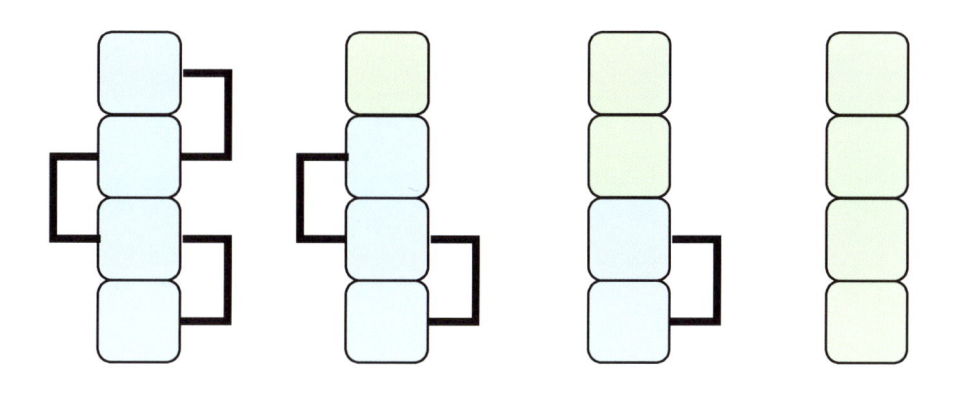

Essential algorithms for A level Computer Science

Stepping through the bubble sort

Index:	0	1	2	3	4
Step 1	Compare Florida and Georgia. No swap needed.					
	→Florida	Georgia←	Delaware	Alabama	California
Step 2	Compare Georgia and Delaware. Swap the items.					
	Florida	→Georgia	Delaware←	Alabama	California
Step 3	Compare Georgia and Alabama. Swap the items.					
	Florida	Delaware	→Georgia	Alabama←	California
Step 4	Compare Georgia and California. Swap the items.					
	Florida	Delaware	Alabama	→Georgia	California←
Step 5	Georgia has bubbled to the end of the list. Start the algorithm again because at least one swap was made. Compare Florida with Delaware. Swap the items.				
	→Florida	Delaware←	Alabama	California	Georgia
Step 6	Compare Florida with Alabama. Swap the items.				
	Delaware	→Florida	Alabama←	California	Georgia
Step 7	Compare Florida with California. Swap the items.				
	Delaware	Alabama	→Florida	California←	Georgia
Step 8	Florida has bubbled to the end of the list. Start the algorithm again because at least one swap was made. Compare Delaware with Alabama. Swap the items.				
	→Delaware	Alabama←	California	Florida	Georgia
Step 9	Compare Delaware with California. Swap the items.				
	Alabama	→Delaware	California←	Florida	Georgia

Step 10	Delaware has bubbled to the end of the list. Start the algorithm again because at least one swap was made. Compare Alabama with California. No swap needed.				
	→Alabama	California←	Delaware	Florida	Georgia
Step 11	No swaps were made, the list is sorted.				
	Alabama	California	Delaware	Florida	Georgia

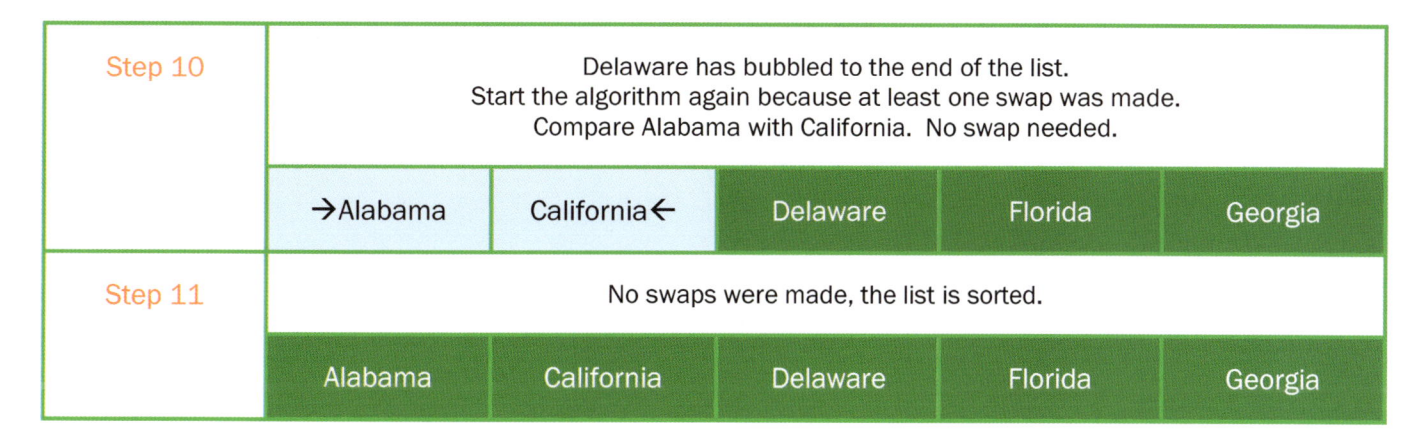

Pseudocode for the bubble sort

```
items = ["Florida","Georgia","Delaware","Alabama","California"]
n = items.Length
swapped = True
While n > 0 AND swapped
        swapped = False
        n = n - 1
        For index = 0 TO n - 1
                If items[index] > items[index+1] then
                        Swap(items[index], items[index+1])
                        swapped = True
                End If
        End For
End while
```

Bubble sort coded in Python

```python
items = ["Florida","Georgia","Delaware","Alabama","California"]
n = len(items)
swapped = True
while n > 0 and swapped == True:
    swapped = False
    n = n - 1
    for index in range(0,n):
        if items[index] > items[index+1]:
            temp = items[index]
            items[index] = items[index+1]
            items[index+1]  =temp
            swapped = True
#Output the result
print(items)
```

Essential algorithms for A level Computer Science

Bubble sort coded in Visual Basic Console

```vb
Module Module1
    Sub Main()
        Dim items() As String = {"Florida", "California", "Delaware", "Alabama", "Georgia"}
        Dim n As Integer = items.Count
        Dim index As Integer
        Dim swapped As Boolean = True
        Dim temp As String
        While n > 0 And swapped = True
            swapped = False
            n = n - 1
            For index = 0 To n - 1
                If items(index) > items(index + 1) Then
                    temp = items(index)
                    items(index) = items(index + 1)
                    items(index + 1) = temp
                    swapped = True
                End If
            Next
        End While
        'Output
        Console.WriteLine(String.Join(", ", items))
        Console.ReadLine()
    End Sub
End Module
```

Did you know?

The bubble sort is also called the "sinking sort." Although it is regarded as an inefficient sorting algorithm, it is a good solution if a data set is almost sorted already. It has an advantage over the merge sort and quicksort because it can detect when the sort is complete. This can make it more efficient in some situations.

Efficiency of the bubble sort

Time complexity			Space complexity
Best case	Average case	Worst case	
O(n)	O(n²)	O(n²)	O(1)
Linear	Polynomial	Polynomial	Constant

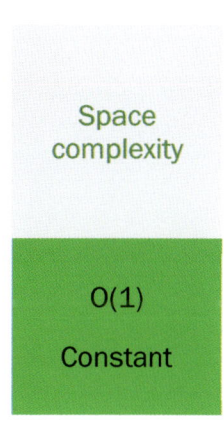

In the best case, the data set is already ordered — in which case, only one pass is required to check all the items in the list and no swaps will be made. Therefore, it is of linear complexity: O(n). This is not usually the case, as the purpose of the algorithm is to sort data.

As the algorithm contains a nested loop, it usually has polynomial complexity — O(n²) — because the time it takes to execute both iterations increases with the size of the data set. However, it does not require any additional memory. It can be performed on the data structure containing the data set, so the space complexity is O(1).

The most efficient method of implementing a bubble sort stops the algorithm when no swaps are made. Although this is not necessary, it is preferable and reduces execution time.

Did you know?

There have been attempts to improve the efficiency of the bubble sort. One includes reversing the direction of the algorithm after each iteration. This is known as a "cocktail sort." The "comb sort" is another method that compares non-adjacent items. At best, a comb sort can perform as well as a quicksort.

Essential algorithms for A level Computer Science

Insertion sort

The insertion sort inserts each item into its correct position in a data set one at a time. It is a useful algorithm for small data sets.

Applications of an insertion sort

The insertion sort is particularly useful for inserting items into an already sorted list. It is usually replaced by more efficient sorting algorithms for large data sets.

Craig'n'Dave video

https://www.craigndave.org/algorithm-insertion-sort

Insertion sort in simple-structured English

1. Start at the second item in the list.

2. Compare current item with the first item in the sorted list.

3. If the current item is greater than the item in the list, move to the next item in the sorted list.

4. Repeat from step 3 until the position of the current item is less than or equal to the item in the sorted list.

5. Move all the items in the list from the current position up one place to create a space for the current item.

6. Insert the current item.

7. Repeat from step 2 with the next item in the list until all the items have been inserted.

Sorting algorithms

Insertion sort illustrated

If illustrations help you remember, this is how you can picture an insertion sort:

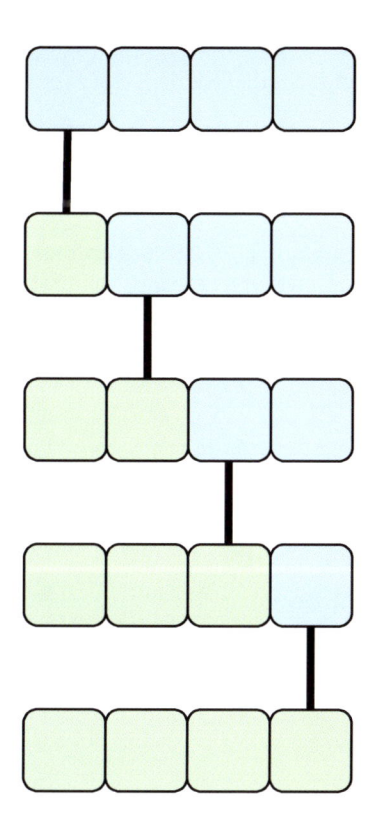

Did you know?

The insertion sort can out-perform a quicksort on small data sets, so it is often used as an optimisation of a quicksort. Once the number of items in a list becomes small, an efficient quicksort will execute an insertion sort on the smaller list instead.

Essential algorithms for A level Computer Science

Stepping through the insertion sort

Index:	0	1	2	3	4
Step 1	\multicolumn{5}{c}{Start at the second item (index 1): Georgia. Compare Georgia with the first item in the list: Florida.}
	→Florida	Georgia←	Delaware	Alabama	California
Step 2	\multicolumn{5}{c}{Georgia is greater than Florida. It is in the correct place. Move to the next item: Delaware. Compare Delaware with the first item in the list: Florida}
	→Florida	Georgia	Delaware←	Alabama	California
Step 3	\multicolumn{5}{c}{Delaware is less than Florida. Insert before Florida. Move to the next item: Alabama. Compare Alabama with the first item in the list: Delaware.}
	→Delaware	Florida	Georgia	Alabama←	California
Step 4	\multicolumn{5}{c}{Alabama is less than Delaware. Insert before Delaware. Move to the next item: California. Compare California with the first item in the list: Alabama.}
	→Alabama	Delaware	Florida	Georgia	California←
Step 5	\multicolumn{5}{c}{California is greater than Alabama. Check the next item in the list: Delaware}
	Alabama	→Delaware	Florida	Georgia	California←
Step 6	\multicolumn{5}{c}{California is less than Delaware. Insert California.}
	Alabama	California	Delaware	Florida	Georgia
	\multicolumn{5}{c}{No more items in the list to check. Sort complete.}

SORTING ALGORITHMS

Pseudocode for the insertion sort

```
items = ["Florida","Georgia","Delaware","Alabama","California"]
For index = 1 TO items.Length:
      index2 = index - 1
      While index2 > 0 AND items[index2 -1] > items[index]
            items[index2] = items[index2 -1]
            index2 = index2 -1
      End while
      items[index2] = items[index]
End For
```

Insertion sort coded in Python

```python
items = ["Florida","Georgia","Delaware","Alabama","California"]
n = len(items)
for index in range(1,n):
    current = items[index]
    index2 = index
    while index2 > 0 and items[index2 -1] > current:
        items[index2] = items[index2 -1]
        index2 = index2 -1
    items[index2] = current
#Output the result
print(items)
```

Insertion sort coded in Visual Basic Console

```vb
Module Module1
    Sub Main()
        Dim items() As String = {"Florida", "Georgia", "Delaware", "Alabama", "California"}
        Dim n As Integer = items.Count
        Dim index, index2 As Integer
        Dim current As String
        For index = 1 To n - 1
            current = items(index)
            index2 = index
            While index2 > 0 AndAlso items(index2 - 1) > current
                items(index2) = items(index2 - 1)
                index2 = index2 - 1
            End While
        Next
        'Output
        Console.WriteLine(String.Join(", ", items))
        Console.ReadLine()
    End Sub
End Module
```

127

Essential algorithms for A level Computer Science

Efficiency of the insertion sort

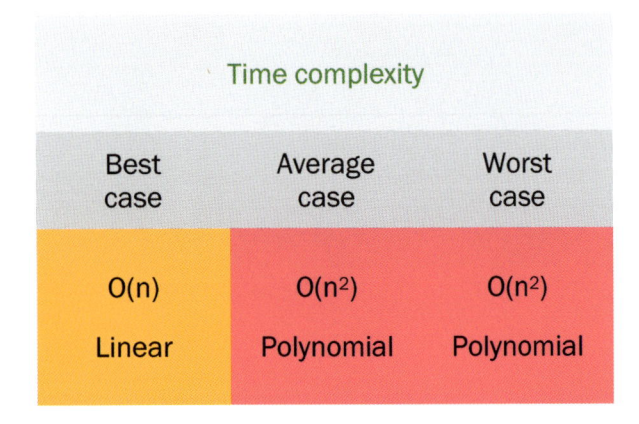

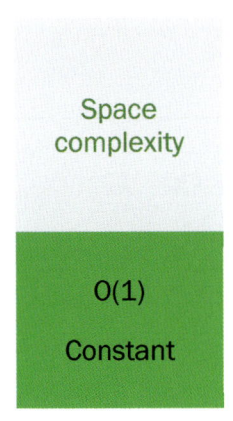

Time complexity			Space complexity
Best case	Average case	Worst case	
$O(n)$ Linear	$O(n^2)$ Polynomial	$O(n^2)$ Polynomial	$O(1)$ Constant

In the best case, the data set is already ordered, so no data needs to be moved. The algorithm has a linear time complexity — $O(n)$ — since each item must still be checked. This is not usually the case, as the purpose of the algorithm is to sort data.

The algorithm contains a nested iteration — one loop to check each item and another to move items so that an item can be slotted into place. Due to these iterations, the algorithm has polynomial complexity: $O(n^2)$.

The algorithm does not require any additional memory, as it can be performed on the data structure containing the data set. Therefore it has a space complexity of $O(1)$.

An alternative version of the algorithm puts sorted data into a new list instead of working on the original list. This does not change the time complexity of the algorithm but would increase the space complexity to $O(n)$.

Did you know?

Attempts have been made to further optimise the insertion sort. "Shellsort," invented in 1959 by Douglas Shell, was the most notable, achieving significantly better performance.

Another optimisation uses a linked list instead of an array, negating the need to move items within the data structure. (See higher order data structures).

Merge sort

A merge sort can sort a data set extremely quickly using **divide and conquer**. The principle of divide and conquer is to create two or more identical sub-problems from the larger problem, solving them individually and combining their solutions to solve the bigger problem. With the merge sort, the data set is repeatedly split in half until each item is in its own list. Adjacent lists are then merged back together, with each item in the sub-list being entered into the correct place in the new, combined list.

Applications of a merge sort

The merge sort is suitable for any data set but works best with larger ones where memory usage is not a concern. However, the time taken to perform the sort should be minimised. It is ideal for parallel processing environments where the concept of divide and conquer can be used.

Craig'n'Dave videos

https://www.craigndave.org/algorithm-merge-sort

Merge sort in simple-structured English

1. Repeatedly divide the list in half into two smaller lists until each item is in its own list.
2. Take two adjacent lists and start with the first item in each one.
3. Compare the two items.
4. Insert the lowest item into a new list. Move to the next item in the list it was taken from.
5. Repeat step 4 until all the items from one of the lists have been put into the new list.
6. Append all the items from the list still containing items to the new list.
7. Remove both old lists.
8. Repeat from step 2 until only one list remains.

When programming this algorithm using iteration, step 1 can be achieved by putting each item into a new list one at a time. This is a simple optimisation that is worth implementing. Examiners will expect you to understand the data set is repeatedly split until each item is in it's own list.

Essential algorithms for A level Computer Science

Merge sort illustrated

If illustrations help you remember, this is how you can picture a merge sort:

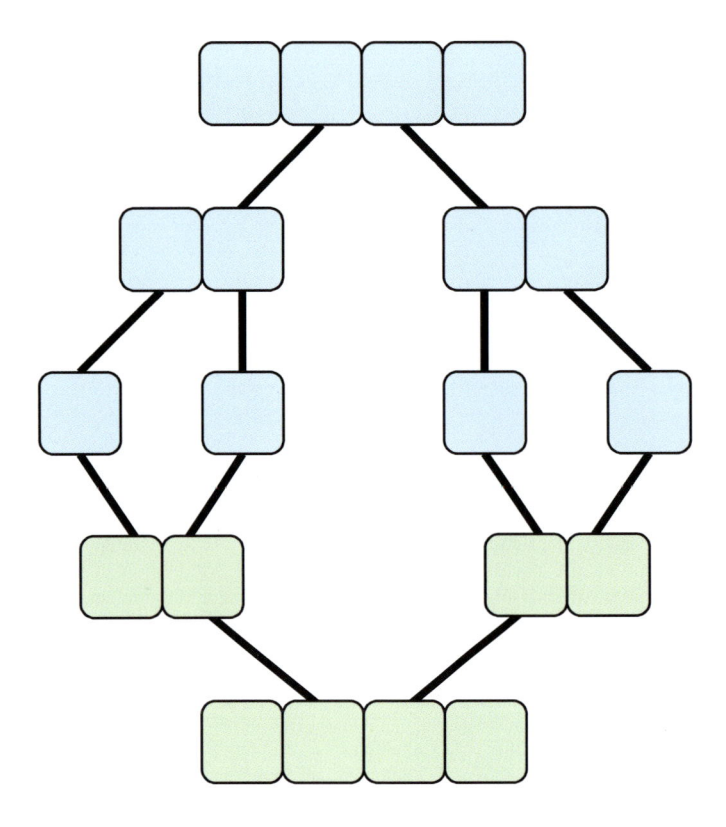

Did you know?

The merge sort is very expensive in terms of space complexity because it repeatedly creates new lists. Most optimisations have explored reducing the amount of memory the algorithm requires.

Stepping through the merge sort

Index:	0	1	2	3	4
Step 1 Split	\multicolumn{5}{c}{Divide the list in half to create two smaller lists.}
	Florida	Georgia	Delaware	Alabama	California
Step 2 Split	\multicolumn{5}{c}{Divide the two lists in half to create four smaller lists.}
	Florida	Georgia	Delaware	Alabama	California
Step 3 Split	\multicolumn{5}{c}{Divide the four lists to create five lists.}
	Florida	Georgia	Delaware	Alabama	California
Step 4 Merge	\multicolumn{5}{c}{Compare Florida to Georgia and merge to one list.}
	Florida	Georgia	Delaware	Alabama	California
Step 5 Merge	\multicolumn{5}{c}{Compare Delaware to Alabama and merge to one list.}
	Florida	Georgia	Alabama	Delaware	California
Step 6 Merge	\multicolumn{5}{c}{Compare Florida to Alabama and merge one item. Compare Delaware to Florida and merge one item. Append all items from remaining list (Florida and Georgia).}
	Alabama	Delaware	Florida	Georgia	California
Step 7 Merge	\multicolumn{5}{c}{Compare Alabama to California and merge one item. Compare Delaware to California and merge one item. Append all items from remaining list (Delaware, Florida and Georgia).}
	Alabama	California	Delaware	Florida	Georgia

Essential algorithms for A level Computer Science

Pseudocode for the merge sort

```
items = ["Florida","Georgia","Delaware","Alabama","California"]
While list_of_items.Length != 1
        index = 0
        While index < list_of_items.Length - 1
                list_of_items = merge(list_of_items[index],list_of_items[index+1])
                index = index + 1
        End while
End while


Function merge(list1,list2)
    newlist = []
    index1 = 0
    index2 = 0
    While index1 < list.Length and index2 < list2.Length
        If list1[index1] > list2[index2] Then
            newlist.append list2[index2]
            index2 = index2 + 1
        ElseIf list1[index1] < list2[index2] Then
            newlist.append list1[index1]
            index1 = index1 + 1
        ElseIf list1[index1] == list2[index2] Then
            newlist.append list1[index1]
            newlist.append list2[index2]
            index1 = index1 + 1
            index2 = index2 + 1
        End If
    If index1 < list1.Length Then
        For item = index1 to list1.Length
            newlist.append list1[item]
        Next item
    ElseIf index2 < list2.Length Then
        For item = index2 to list2.Length
            newlist.append list2[item]
        Next item
    Return newlist
```

Merge sort coded in Python using iteration

```python
def merge(list1, list2):
    #Function to merge two lists into a new list
    newlist = []
    index1 = 0
    index2 = 0
    #Check each item in each list, and add the smallest item to a new list
    while index1 < len(list1) and index2 < len(list2):
        if list1[index1] > list2[index2]:
            newlist.append(list2[index2])
            index2 = index2 + 1
        elif list1[index1] < list2[index2]:
            newlist.append(list1[index1])
            index1 = index1 + 1
        elif list1[index1] == list2[index2]:
            newlist.append(list1[index1])
            newlist.append(list2[index2])
            index1 = index1 + 1
            index2 = index2 + 1
    #Add left over items from the remaining list
    if index1 < len(list1):
        for item in range(index1, len(list1)):
            newlist.append(list1[item])
    elif index2 < len(list2):
        for item in range(index2, len(list2)):
            newlist.append(list2[item])
    return newlist

#Main algorithm starts here
items = ["Florida","Georgia","Delaware","Alabama","California"]
listofitems = []
#Every item is put into it's own list within a container list
for n in range(len(items)):
    item = [items[n]]
    listofitems.append(item)
#Repeat while there is more than one list
while len(listofitems) != 1:
    index = 0
    #Merge pairs of lists
    while index < len(listofitems)-1:
        newlist = merge(listofitems[index], listofitems[index+1])
        listofitems[index] = newlist
        #Once merged, delete one of the now redundant lists
        del listofitems[index+1]
        index = index + 1

#Output
print(listofitems[0])
```

Merge sort coded in Visual Basic Console using iteration

```vb
Module Module1
    Function merge(list1 As List(Of String), list2 As List(Of String))
        'Function to merge two lists into a new list
        Dim newlist As New List(Of String)
        Dim index1 As Integer = 0
        Dim index2 As Integer = 0
        'Check Each item In Each list, and add the smallest item To a new list
        Do While index1 < list1.Count And index2 < list2.Count
            If list1(index1) > list2(index2) Then
                newlist.Add(list2(index2))
                index2 = index2 + 1
            ElseIf list1(index1) < list2(index2) Then
                newlist.Add(list1(index1))
                index1 = index1 + 1
            ElseIf list1(index1) = list2(index2) Then
                newlist.Add(list1(index1))
                newlist.Add(list2(index2))
                index1 = index1 + 1
                index2 = index2 + 1
            End If
        Loop

        'Add left over items from the remaining list
        If index1 < list1.Count Then
            For item = index1 To list1.Count - 1
                newlist.Add(list1(item))
            Next
        ElseIf index2 < list2.Count Then
            For item = index2 To list2.Count - 1
                newlist.Add(list2(item))
            Next
        End If

        Return newlist
    End Function

    'Main algorithm starts here
    Sub Main()
        Dim items() As String = {"Florida", "Georgia", "Delaware", "Alabama", "California"}
        Dim listofitems As New List(Of List(Of String))
        Dim newlist As List(Of String)
        Dim item As List(Of String)
        Dim index As Integer
        'Every item is put into it's own list within a container list
        For n = 0 To items.Count - 1
            item = New List(Of String)
            item.Add(items(n))
```

```vbnet
            listofitems.Add(item)
        Next

        'Repeat while there is more than one list
        Do While listofitems.Count <> 1
            index = 0
            'Merge pairs of lists
            Do While index < listofitems.Count - 1
                newlist = merge(listofitems(index), listofitems(index + 1))
                listofitems(index) = newlist
                'Once merged, delete one of the now redundant lists
                listofitems.RemoveAt(index + 1)
                index = index + 1
            Loop
        Loop
        'Output
        For index = 0 To listofitems(0).Count - 1
            Console.WriteLine(listofitems(0)(index))
        Next
        Console.ReadLine()
    End Sub
End Module
```

Efficiency of the merge sort

Time complexity			Space complexity
Best case	Average case	Worst case	
O(n log n)	O(n log n)	O(n log n)	O(n)
Linearithmic	Linearithmic	Linearithmic	Linear

In all cases, the data in a merge sort needs to be manipulated so that each item is in it's own list. The time this takes will increase with more data, and so too will the memory requirements: O(n). However, by using a divide and conquer algorithm, the data set can be repeatedly divided: O(log n).

When the lists are merged back together, it is possible to merge more than one list simultaneously, although each item in the list needs to be considered in turn to determine its position in the new list. Therefore, the algorithm has a linearithmic time complexity — O(n log n) — and a space complexity of O(n).

Essential algorithms for A level Computer Science

An alternative implementation using recursion

While it is more memory-efficient to implement the merge sort using iteration alone, the algorithm can be optimised for parallel processing using recursion.

An alternative implementation using recursion in Python

```python
def mergeSort(items):
    print("Splitting ",items)
    if len(items)>1:
        mid=len(items)//2
        lefthalf=items[:mid]
        righthalf=items[mid:]

        mergeSort(lefthalf)
        mergeSort(righthalf)

        i=0
        j=0
        k=0
        print("Merging ",items)
        while i < len(lefthalf) and j <len(righthalf):
            if lefthalf[i]<righthalf[j]:
                items[k]=lefthalf[i]
                i=i+1
            else:
                items[k]=righthalf[j]
                j=j+1
            k=k+1

        while i <len(lefthalf):
            items[k]=lefthalf[i]
            i=i+1
            k=k+1

        while j<len(righthalf):
            items[k]=righthalf[j]
            j=j+1
            k=k+1

items = ["Florida","Georgia","Delaware","Alabama","California"]
mergeSort(items)
print(items)
```

An alternative implementation using recursion in Visual Basic Console

```vb
Module Module1
    Function merge(list1 As List(Of String), list2 As List(Of String))
        'Function to merge two lists into a new list
        Dim newlist As New List(Of String)
        Dim index1 As Integer = 0
        Dim index2 As Integer = 0
        'Check Each item In Each list, and add the smallest item To a new list
        Do While index1 < list1.Count And index2 < list2.Count
            If list1(index1) > list2(index2) Then
                newlist.Add(list2(index2))
                index2 = index2 + 1
            ElseIf list1(index1) < list2(index2) Then
                newlist.Add(list1(index1))
                index1 = index1 + 1
            ElseIf list1(index1) = list2(index2) Then
                newlist.Add(list1(index1))
                newlist.Add(list2(index2))
                index1 = index1 + 1
                index2 = index2 + 1
            End If
        Loop

        'Add left over items from the remaining list
        If index1 < list1.Count Then
            For item = index1 To list1.Count - 1
                newlist.Add(list1(item))
            Next
        ElseIf index2 < list2.Count Then
            For item = index2 To list2.Count - 1
                newlist.Add(list2(item))
            Next
        End If

        Return newlist
    End Function

    'Main algorithm starts here
    Sub Main()
        Dim items() As String = {"Florida", "Georgia", "Delaware", "Alabama", "California"}
        Dim listofitems As New List(Of List(Of String))
        Dim newlist As List(Of String)
        Dim item As List(Of String)
        Dim index As Integer
        'Every item is put into it's own list within a container list
        For n = 0 To items.Count - 1
            item = New List(Of String)
            item.Add(items(n))
```

Essential algorithms for A level Computer Science

```vbnet
            listofitems.Add(item)
        Next

        'Repeat while there is more than one list
        Do While listofitems.Count <> 1
            index = 0
            'Merge pairs of lists
            Do While index < listofitems.Count - 1
                newlist = merge(listofitems(index), listofitems(index + 1))
                listofitems(index) = newlist
                'Once merged, delete one of the now redundant lists
                listofitems.RemoveAt(index + 1)
                index = index + 1
            Loop
        Loop
        'Output
        For index = 0 To listofitems(0).Count - 1
            Console.WriteLine(listofitems(0)(index))
        Next
        Console.ReadLine()
    End Sub
End Module
```

Did you know?

The merge sort was extremely popular in the early days of computer science because the algorithm could be run on multiple tape drives. Modern solid state drives and even magnetic hard disks allow for any item of data on the drive to be randomly accessed. However, with tape drives, data could only be accessed serially, one item at a time.

Quicksort

Perhaps not unsurprisingly given the name of the algorithm, the quicksort orders a data set extremely quickly using **divide and conquer**. The principle of divide and conquer is to create two or more identical, smaller sub-problems from the larger problem, before solving them individually and combining their solutions to solve the bigger problem. The algorithm makes use a of a pivot value from the data set, against which other items are compared to determine their position. It is often considered more efficient than a merge sort due to requiring less memory than a typical recursive merge sort implementation, but this is not really the case. It is usually dependent on the factors affecting the algorithm such as the data set being sorted and the pivot chosen.

Applications of a quicksort

The quicksort is suitable for any data set but shines with larger data sets. It is ideal for parallel processing environments where the concept of divide and conquer can be used. Typically found in real-time situations due to its efficiency, the quicksort has applications in medical monitoring, life support systems, aircraft controls and defence systems.

Craig'n'Dave video

https://www.craigndave.org/algorithms-quick-sort

Quick sort in simple-structured English

A pivot item is chosen, against which other items will be compared. This is usually the first item in the list, although it can be any item, including the last, or a random item. Two pointers are each compared with the pivot in turn until the correct position for the pivot is determined. The algorithm is then repeated recursively on the items to the left and right of this position.

This approach can be described with the following pseudocode:

1. Set the pivot value as the first item in the list.

2. Set a pointer to the second and last items in the list.

3. While the second pointer is greater than or equal to the first pointer:

    a. Whilst the first pointer is less than or equal to the second pointer and the item at the first pointer is less than or equal to the pivot value, increase the first pointer by one.

    b. Whilst the second pointer is greater than or equal to the first pointer and the item at the second pointer is greater than or equal to the pivot, decrease the second pointer by one.

    c. If the second pointer is greater than the first pointer, swap the items.

4. Swap the pivot value with the item at the second pointer.

5. Repeat from step 1 on the list of items to the left of the second pointer.

Essential algorithms for A level Computer Science

6. Repeat from step 1 on the list of items to the right of the second pointer.

Quicksort illustrated

If illustrations help you remember, this is how you can picture a quicksort:

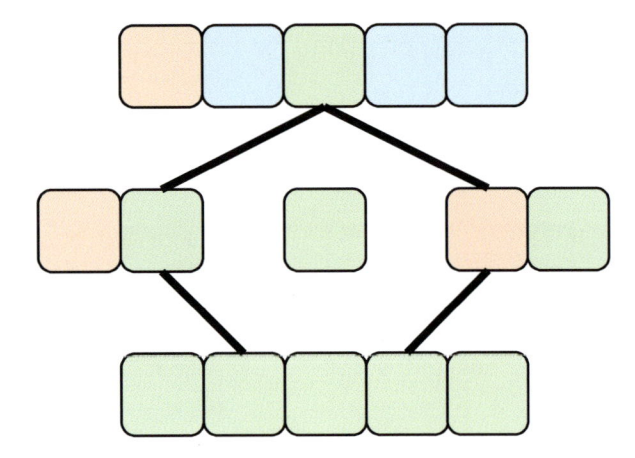

Did you know?

The quicksort was invented by Tony Hoare while he was a student in the Soviet Union. He was working on a machine translation project and needed to sort Russian words, before looking them up in an English-Russian dictionary. Having initially developed the insertion sort, he realised it was too slow and developed the quicksort instead.

When back in England, Tony Hoare was asked to write code for a Shellsort but instead placed a bet that his sorting algorithm was the fastest. He won a sixpence! The quicksort is now a widely adopted sorting algorithm in most programming language libraries today.

Stepping through the quicksort

Index:	0	1	2	3	4
Step 1	Set the pivot to the first item. Set pointers on indexes 1 and 4.					
	Florida	→Georgia	Delaware	Alabama	California←
Step 2	Consider first pointer: Georgia is not less than Florida. First pointer finished.				
	Florida	→Georgia	Delaware	Alabama	California←
Step 3	Consider second pointer: California is less than Florida. Swap Georgia and California.				
	Florida	→California	Delaware	Alabama	Georgia←
Step 4	Consider first pointer: California is less than Florida. Increment the first pointer.				
	Florida	California	→Delaware	Alabama	Georgia←
Step 5	Consider first pointer: Delaware is less than Florida. Increment the first pointer.				
	Florida	California	Delaware	→Alabama←	Georgia
Step 6	Consider first pointer: Alabama is less than Florida. Increment the first pointer.				
	Florida	California	Delaware	Alabama←	→Georgia
Step 7	The first pointer is greater than the second pointer. Swap the pivot value with the second pointer: Alabama and Florida.				
	Alabama	California	Delaware	**Florida**	Georgia
Step 8	Quicksort the items to the left of Florida. Set Alabama as the pivot. Set pointers on indexes 1 and 2.				
	Alabama	→California	Delaware←	**Florida**	Georgia
Step 9	Consider first pointer: California is not less than Alabama. First pointer finished.				
	Alabama	→California	Delaware←	**Florida**	Georgia

141

Essential algorithms for A level Computer Science

Step 10	Consider second pointer: Delaware is greater than Alabama. Decrement second pointer.				
	Alabama ←	→California	Delaware	Florida	Georgia

Step 11	Consider second pointer: California is greater than Alabama. Decrement second pointer.				
	Alabama	→California←	Delaware	Florida	Georgia

Step 12	The first pointer is greater than the second pointer. Swap the pivot value with the second pointer: Alabama and Alabama.				
	Alabama ←	→California	Delaware	Florida	Georgia

Step 13	Quicksort the items to the left of Alabama: none. Quicksort the items to the right of Alabama. Set California as the pivot. Set pointers on indexes 2 and 2.				
	Alabama	California	→Delaware←	Florida	Georgia

Step 14	Consider first pointer: Delaware is not less than California. First pointer finished.				
	Alabama	California	→Delaware←	Florida	Georgia

Step 15	Consider second pointer: Delaware is greater than Alabama. Decrement second pointer.				
	Alabama	California ←	→Delaware	Florida	Georgia

Step 16	The first pointer is greater than the second pointer. Swap the pivot value with the second pointer: California and California.				
	Alabama	California	Delaware	Florida	Georgia

Step 17	Quicksort the items to the left of California: none. Quicksort the items to the right of California: Delaware. Only one item in list. Return Delaware.				
	Alabama	California	Delaware	Florida	Georgia

Step 18	Quicksort the items to the right of Florida: Georgia. Only one item in list. Return Georgia.				
	Alabama	California	Delaware	Florida	Georgia

Pseudocode for the quicksort

```
items = ["Florida","Georgia","Delaware","Alabama","California"]
Function quicksort(list)
      If items.Length <= 1 Then Return items
      pointer1 = 1
      pointer2 = items.Length - 1
      pivot = items[0]
      While pointer2 >= pointer1
            While pointer1 <= pointer2 And items[pointer1] <= pivot
                  pointer1 = pointer1 + 1
            End While
            While pointer2 >= pointer1 And items[pointer2] >= pivot
                  pointer2 = pointer2 - 1
            End While
            If pointer2 > pointer1 Then Swap(items[pointer1],items[pointer2])
      End While
      Swap(pivot,items[pointer2])
      left = quicksort(items[0 to pointer2])
      right = quicksort(items[pointer2 + 1 to items.Length])
      Return left + items[pointer2] + right
End Function
```

Did you know?

The quicksort often causes debate between students of mathematics and computer science because there is more than one way to write a quicksort.

These include Tony Hoare's method — using a pointer that starts at each end of the data set and moves inwards — and the Nico Lomuto method, which starts with a pivot at the end of the data set. Both are valid quicksort algorithms.

You may be more likely to learn the Hoare method in A level computer science and the Lomuto method in A level mathematics.

Quicksort coded in Python

```python
def quicksort(items):
    if len(items) <=1:
        return items
    else:
        pointer1 = 1
        pointer2 = len(items)-1
        pivotvalue = items[0]

        while pointer2 >= pointer1:
            while pointer1 <= pointer2 and items[pointer1] <= pivotvalue:
                pointer1 = pointer1 + 1
            while pointer2 >= pointer1 and items[pointer2] >= pivotvalue:
                pointer2 = pointer2 -1
            if pointer2 > pointer1:
                temp = items[pointer1]
                items[pointer1] = items[pointer2]
                items[pointer2] = temp

        temp = items[0]
        items[0] = items[pointer2]
        items[pointer2] = temp

        left = quicksort(items[0:pointer2])
        right = quicksort(items[pointer2+1:len(items)])

        return left+[items[pointer2]]+right

#Main program starts here
items = ["Florida","Georgia","Delaware","Alabama","California"]
print(quicksort(items))
```

Did you know?

"To what extent is a quicksort suitable for parallel processing?" would be a great examination question. The location of the first item can be found efficiently by one processor but, once the data set is split, two processors can work independently on the two data sets.

Quicksort coded in Visual Basic Console

```vb
Module Module1
    Function quicksort(items As List(Of String))
        If items.Count <= 1 Then Return items
        Dim pointer1 As Integer = 1
        Dim pointer2 As Integer = items.Count - 1
        Dim pivotvalue As String = items(0)
        Dim temp As String

        While pointer2 >= pointer1
            While pointer1 <= pointer2 And items(pointer1) <= pivotvalue
                pointer1 = pointer1 + 1
            End While
            While pointer2 >= pointer1 And items(pointer2) >= pivotvalue
                pointer2 = pointer2 - 1
            End While

            If pointer2 > pointer1 Then
                temp = items(pointer1)
                items(pointer1) = items(pointer2)
                items(pointer2) = temp
            End If
        End While
        temp = items(0)
        items(0) = items(pointer2)
        items(pointer2) = temp

        Dim newlist As New List(Of String)
        newlist.AddRange(quicksort(items.GetRange(0, pointer2)))
        newlist.Add(items(pointer2))
        newlist.AddRange(quicksort(items.GetRange(pointer2 + 1, items.Count() - 1 - pointer2)))

        Return newlist
    End Function

    'Main algorithm starts here
    Sub Main()
        Dim items As New List(Of String) From {"Florida", "Georgia", "Delaware", "Alabama", "California"}
        items = quicksort(items)
        'Output
        Console.WriteLine(String.Join(", ", items))
        Console.ReadLine()
    End Sub
End Module
```

Efficiency of the quicksort

Time complexity			Space complexity
Best case	Average case	Worst case	
O(n log n) Linearithmic	O(n log n) Linearithmic	O(n^2) Polynomial	O(log n) Logarithmic

Once the position of the pivot is found, the quicksort can divide the list in half and recursively solve the quicksort on each of the sub-lists. This makes the algorithm ideal for parallel processing. Dividing the data set in this way provides a linearithmic time complexity: O(n log n). It is unlikely that the data set will be divided equally in half, but in the worst case, the pivot will always be the first or last item, and the time complexity becomes polynomial: O(n^2). At best, the data set will always be divided equally, resulting in linearithmic complexity: O(n log n). On average the position of the pivot item will be somewhere between the first and last item in the data set, and the time complexity averages out.

The code examples presented are not memory-efficient because they create new lists for each recursive call. Implementing the algorithm in this way increases the space complexity but makes the algorithm easier to code and understand. An alternative approach would use the same data set, passing the pointers as parameters and not the data structure to the quicksort function.

However, any recursive algorithm — even if it does not create new data sets — will require a call stack, so the space complexity is still considered O(log n) and not O(1).

One method of further optimising the quicksort is to recognise when the number of items in the data set is small and switch to a more optimal algorithm for small data sets such as an insertion sort.

Did you know?

The quicksort can also be visualised as a binary tree. The root node is the first pivot. The pivot on the left part of the tree is the root of that sub-tree. The pivot on the right part of the tree is the root of that sub-tree.

Alternative method for a quicksort

As with many algorithms, there is often more than one approach that can be taken, due to the limitations of a programming language, different programming paradigms or underlying data structures, employing optimisations, further research and development into the time complexity, or simply because there is more than one valid approach. The quicksort is one such algorithm where there are several similar approaches. This is often confusing for students because mark schemes and other sources may present a different answer to the same algorithm. Providing you show your working, the algorithm will still be recognisable, and you will still gain credit for an alternative approach.

To illustrate the point, this approach uses the last item as the pivot:

1. Set a pointer to the first and last items in the list.
2. Whilst the first pointer is not equal to the second pointer:
   a. If the item at the first pointer is greater than the item at the second pointer, swap the items and the pointers.
   b. Move the first pointer one item towards the second pointer. (Note: this could be a move towards the left or right in the data set. Only one pointer ever moves in this method.)
3. Repeat from step 1 on the list of items to the left of a pointer.
4. Repeat from step 1 on the list of items to the right of a pointer.

Stepping through an alternative quicksort

Index:	0	1	2	3	4
Step 1	Set pointers on indexes 0 and 4. Note: → is the first pointer. ← is the second (pivot) pointer.				
	→Florida	Georgia	Delaware	Alabama	California←
Step 2	Compare Florida and California. Florida is greater than California. Swap items and pointers.				
	California←	Georgia	Delaware	Alabama	→Florida
Step 3	Move the first pointer towards the second pointer.				
	California←	Georgia	Delaware	→Alabama	Florida
Step 4	Compare Alabama with California. Alabama is less than California. Swap items and pointers.				
	→Alabama	Georgia	Delaware	California←	Florida

Essential algorithms for A level Computer Science

Step 5	Move the first pointer towards the second pointer.				
	Alabama	→Georgia	Delaware	California←	Florida
Step 6	Compare Georgia with California. Georgia is greater than California. Swap items and pointers.				
	Alabama	California←	Delaware	→Georgia	Florida
Step 7	Move the first pointer towards the second pointer.				
	Alabama	California←	→Delaware	Georgia	Florida
Step 8	Compare Delaware with California. Delaware is greater than California. No swap needed.				
	Alabama	California←	→Delaware	Georgia	Florida
Step 9	Move the first pointer towards the second pointer.				
	Alabama	→California←	Delaware	Georgia	Florida
Step 10	The pointers are equal. Quicksort items to the left of California. Set pointers on indexes 0 and 0. Since the pointers are equal and there are no left or right lists, this branch of the algorithm is complete.				
	→Alabama←	California	Delaware	Georgia	Florida
Step 11	Quicksort items to the right of California. Set pointers on indexes 2 and 4.				
	Alabama	California	→Delaware	Georgia	Florida←
Step 12	Compare Delaware with Florida. Delaware is less than Florida, no swap needed.				
	Alabama	California	→Delaware	Georgia	Florida←
Step 13	Move the first pointer towards the second pointer.				
	Alabama	California	Delaware	→Georgia	Florida←
Step 14	Compare Georgia with Florida. Georgia is greater than Florida. Swap items and pointers.				
	Alabama	California	Delaware	Florida←	→Georgia

SORTING ALGORITHMS

148

Step 15	Move the first pointer towards the second pointer.					
	Alabama	California	Delaware	→Florida←	Georgia
Step 16	The pointers are equal. Quicksort items to the left of Florida. Set pointers on indexes 2 and 2. Since the pointers are equal and there are no left or right lists, this branch of the algorithm is complete.					
	Alabama	California	→Delaware←	Florida	Georgia
Step 17	Quicksort items to the right of Florida. Set pointers on indexes 4 and 4. Since the pointers are equal and there are no left or right lists, this branch of the algorithm is complete.					
	Alabama	California	Delaware	Florida	→Georgia←

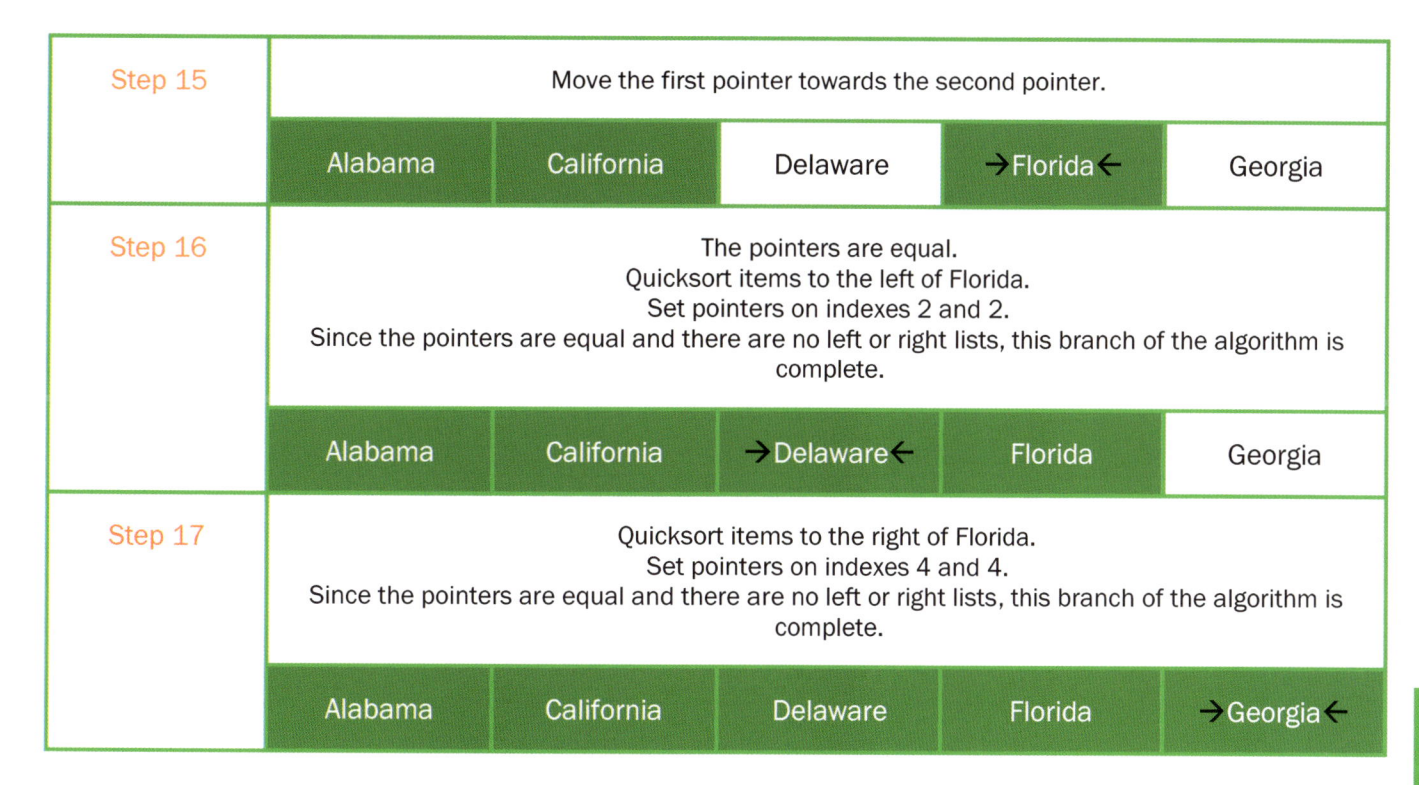

Pseudocode for an alternative quicksort

```
items = ["Florida","Georgia","Delaware","Alabama","California"]
Function quicksort(list)
      If items.Length <= 1 Then Return items
      pointer1 = 0
      While pointer1 != pointer2
            If (items[pointer1] > items[pointer2] and pointer1 < pointer2) or (items[pointer1] < items[pointer2] and pointer1 > pointer2) Then
                  Swap(items[pointer1],items[pointer2])
                  Swap(pointer1, pointer2)
            End If
            If pointer1 < pointer2 Then
                  pointer1 = pointer1 + 1
            Else
                  pointer1 = pointer1 - 1
            End If
      End While
      left = quicksort(items[0 to pointer1])
      right = quicksort(items[pointer1 + 1 to items.Length])
      Return left + items[pointer1] + right
End Function
```

An alternative quicksort coded in Python

```python
def quicksort(items):
    if len(items) <= 1:
        return items
    else:
        pointer1 = 0
        pointer2 = len(items)-1

        while pointer1 != pointer2:
            if (items[pointer1] > items[pointer2] and pointer1 < pointer2) or (items[pointer1] < items[pointer2] and pointer1 > pointer2):
                temp = items[pointer1]
                items[pointer1] = items[pointer2]
                items[pointer2] = temp
                temp_pointer = pointer1
                pointer1 = pointer2
                pointer2 = temp_pointer
            if pointer1 < pointer2:
                pointer1 = pointer1 + 1
            else:
                pointer1 = pointer1 - 1

        left = quicksort(items[0:pointer1])
        right = quicksort(items[pointer1+1:len(items)])

        return left+[items[pointer1]]+right

#Main program starts here
items = ["Florida","Georgia","Delaware","Alabama","California"]
print(quicksort(items))
```

> ### Did you know?
>
> One of the goals of a good sorting algorithm is not to change the order of items that are the same. This is often useful in operations such as sorting file names on a disk and presenting them to a user — a typical operation for an operating system. Moving items unnecessarily is called **instability** and is a weakness of the quicksort.

An alternative quicksort coded in Visual Basic Console

```vb
Module Module1
    Function quicksort(items As List(Of String))
        If items.Count <= 1 Then Return items
        Dim pointer1 As Integer = 0
        Dim pointer2 As Integer = items.Count - 1
        Dim temp, temp_pointer As String

        While pointer1 <> pointer2
            If (items(pointer1) > items(pointer2) And pointer1 < pointer2) Or (items(pointer1) < items(pointer2) And pointer1 > pointer2) Then
                temp = items(pointer1)
                items(pointer1) = items(pointer2)
                items(pointer2) = temp
                temp_pointer = pointer1
                pointer1 = pointer2
                pointer2 = temp_pointer
            End If
            If pointer1 < pointer2 Then
                pointer1 = pointer1 + 1
            Else
                pointer2 = pointer2 + 1
            End If
        End While

        Dim newlist As New List(Of String)
        newlist.AddRange(quicksort(items.GetRange(0, pointer1)))
        newlist.Add(items(pointer2))
        newlist.AddRange(quicksort(items.GetRange(pointer1 + 1, items.Count() - 1 - pointer1)))

        Return newlist
    End Function

    'Main algorithm starts here
    Sub Main()
        Dim items As New List(Of String) From {"Florida", "Georgia", "Delaware", "Alabama", "California"}
        items = quicksort(items)
        'Output
        Console.WriteLine(String.Join(", ", items))
        Console.ReadLine()
    End Sub
End Module
```

Why are there so many sorting algorithms?

It is easy to jump to the conclusion that there must be a "best" sorting algorithm. While it is true that sorting algorithms have developed over time and research is still ongoing today, there is no "best" sorting algorithm. Each algorithm's performance depends on the data set it is being applied to.

When writing algorithms, there are four significant factors to consider:

1. The processing architecture. Parallel processors usually execute more efficiently than single processors. If a data set can be divided and the same algorithm applied to each sub-set of data, it is well suited to parallelism. Good examples of this are the merge sort and quicksort, which take advantage of divide and conquer and work best with large, unsorted data sets.

2. The memory footprint. The amount of memory an algorithm has to work with can be a limiting factor. In computer science, there is often a balance between the efficiency of processing and the efficiency of memory. In the past, memory was a significant limiting factor, and programmers would strive to save every byte they could. Today, we take for granted the fact we have gigabytes of memory. In the past, computers had only kilobytes of memory to store the operating system, program and data. Algorithms that perform well in a defined memory space include the bubble sort and insertion sort.

3. The volume of code. More efficient algorithms usually require more complex code. This is difficult to write for novice programmers and requires more memory to store. Sometimes, the speed of execution is not the most important factor. A good example of this is the bubble sort, which is easy to write and requires very few lines of code.

4. The state of the data set. Some algorithms that are often less efficient can outperform others if the data set is already partially sorted. A good example of this is the bubble sort. It can outperform a quicksort on a partially sorted list, but it is quickly beaten if the data set is large and random.

It would be a great exercise to take the code for each algorithm in this book and apply it to different types of data sets to see how the speed of execution is affected. Different data sets might include ordered, reverse ordered, random, small and large volumes of data.

Did you know?

In 2001, recognising that no one algorithm is best, Tim Peters invented the Timsort, which is used by the Python sort() method. It is now the default algorithm in Java and across the Android platform. The Timsort is different from other algorithms in that it pre-processes the data to compute which algorithm would be most efficient before applying it. If the array or list has less than 64 elements, it uses an insertion sort. If the data set has more than 64 elements, it uses a variation of a merge sort.

In summary

Bubble sort	Insertion sort	Merge sort	Quicksort
Adjacent items are compared and swapped if they are out of order	Each item is compared to every other item from the start until its place is found	Items in one list are compared to items in another list to create a new list	Items are compared to a pivot
Uses a nested iteration	Uses a nested iteration	Uses either a nested iteration or recursion	Uses either a nested iteration or recursion
Slow	Slow	Quick	Quick
Suitable for a small number of items	Suitable for a small number of items	Suitable for a large number of items	Suitable for a large number of items
Easy to program	Easy to program	More difficult to program	More difficult to program
Known memory footprint	Known memory footprint	Memory footprint can increase as the algorithm executes	Memory footprint can increase as the algorithm executes

OPTIMISATION ALGORITHMS

Routines that find satisfactory or optimum paths between vertices on a graph.

Optimisation algorithms

Dijkstra's shortest path

Dijkstra's shortest path algorithm finds the shortest path between one node and all other nodes on a weighted graph. It is sometimes considered a special case of the A* algorithm with no heuristics, although Edsger Dijkstra developed his algorithm first. It is also a type of breadth-first search. A limitation of Dijkstra's shortest path is that it doesn't work for edges with a negative weight value. The Bellman–Ford algorithm later provided a solution to that problem.

Exam board clarification

For OCR, candidates do not need to be able to code Dijkstra's shortest path. They need to know how it works, calculate the shortest path using the algorithm, and read and trace code that performs the algorithm.

For AQA, candidates do not need to be able to code or recall the steps of Dijkstra's shortest path. They need to understand and trace the algorithm and be aware of its applications.

Applications of Dijkstra's shortest path

Edsger Dijkstra developed his algorithm to find the shortest route of travel between Rotterdam and Groningen. It can be used for many purposes where the shortest path between two points need to be established. Maps, IP routing and the telephone network make use of Dijkstra's algorithm.

Craig'n'Dave videos

https://www.craigndave.org/algorithm-dijkstras-shortest-path

Did you know?

Dijkstra's algorithm was used to demonstrate the computing ability of the new ARMAC computer in 1956. The computer was able to find the shortest routes between 64 cities in the Netherlands on a transport map. 64 was the limit because it only required six bits (2^6) to encode a city name as a number.

Essential algorithms for A level Computer Science

Dijkstra's shortest path in simple-structured English

To calculate the shortest path:

1. For each node in the graph:
   a. Find the node with the shortest distance from the start that has not been visited.
   b. For each connected node that has not been visited:
      i. Calculate the distance from the start.
      ii. If the distance from the start is lower than the currently recorded distance from the start:
         1. Set the shortest distance to the start of the connected node to the newly calculated distance.
         2. Set the previous node to be the current node.
2. Set the node as visited.

To output the shortest path:

3. Start from a goal node
4. Add the previous node to the start of a list.
5. Repeat from step 7 until the start node is reached.
6. Output the list.

Dijkstra's shortest path illustrated

If illustrations help you remember, this is how you can picture Dijkstra's shortest path:

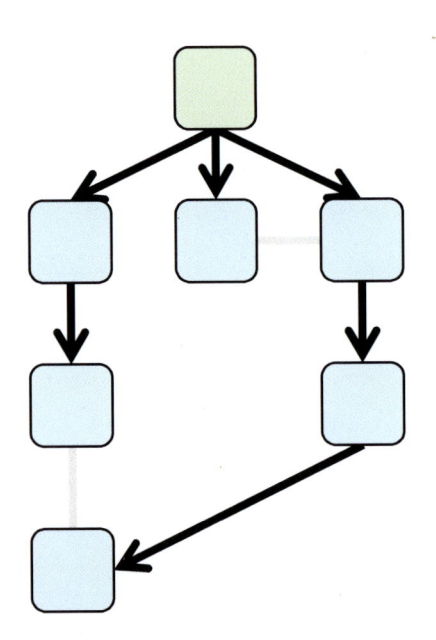

Stepping through Dijkstra's shortest path

| Step 1 | Set the distance from the start for all nodes to infinity. Set the distance from the start for node A to zero. Select the node with the lowest distance from the start that has not been visited: A. Consider each edge from A that has not been visited: B, C, D. |

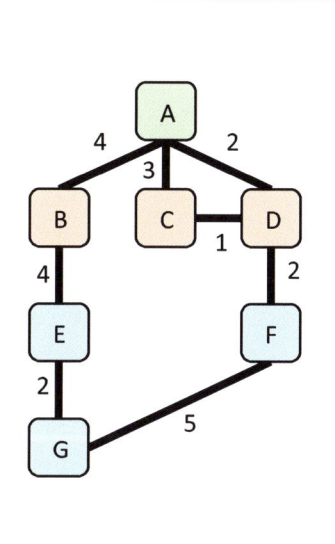

Node	Distance from start	Visited	Previous Node
A	0	No	
B	∞	No	
C	∞	No	
D	∞	No	
E	∞	No	
F	∞	No	
G	∞	No	

| Step 2 | Distance from the start = A's distance from the start + edge weight. B: 0 + 4 = 4 (lower than ∞) – update. C: 0 + 3 = 3 (lower than ∞) – update. D: 0 + 2 = 2 (lower than ∞) - update. Set A to visited. |

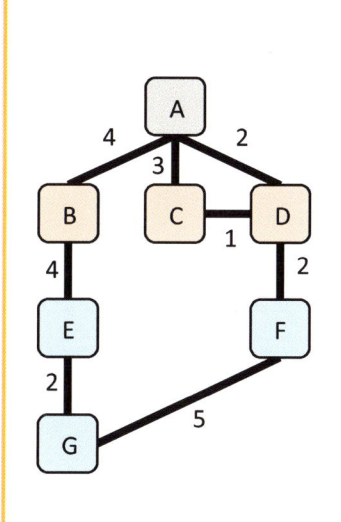

Node	Distance from start	Visited	Previous Node
A	0	Yes	
B	4	No	A
C	3	No	A
D	2	No	A
E	∞	No	
F	∞	No	
G	∞	No	

157

Essential algorithms for A level Computer Science

Step 3	Select the node with the lowest distance from the start that has not been visited: D. Consider each edge from D that has not been visited: C, F.

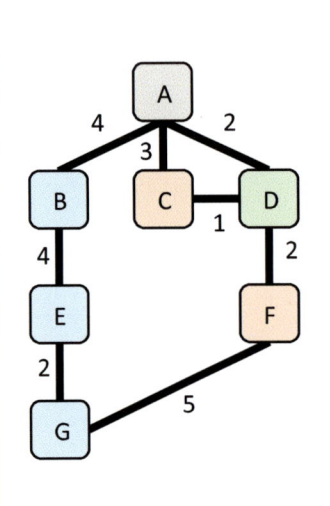

Node	Distance from start	Visited	Previous Node
A	0	Yes	
B	4	No	A
C	3	No	A
D	2	No	A
E	∞	No	
F	∞	No	
G	∞	No	

Step 4	Distance from the start = D's distance from the start + edge weight. C: 2 + 1 = 3 could be updated since the distance to C from A or D is the same, but as the distance from the start is not less than 3, this won't be updated. F: 2 + 2 = 4 (lower than ∞) – update. Set D to visited.

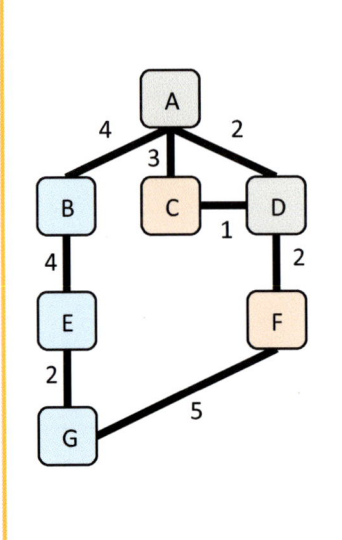

Node	Distance from start	Visited	Previous Node
A	0	Yes	
B	4	No	A
C	3	No	A
D	2	Yes	A
E	∞	No	
F	4	No	D
G	∞	No	

Optimisation algorithms

| Step 5 | Select the node with the lowest distance from the start that has not been visited: C. Consider each edge from C that has not been visited: none. |

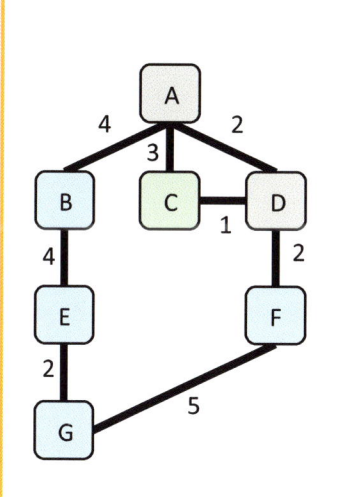

Node	Distance from start	Visited	Previous Node
A	0	Yes	
B	4	No	A
C	3	No	A
D	2	Yes	A
E	∞	No	
F	4	No	D
G	∞	No	

| Step 6 | No edges to consider. Set C to visited. |

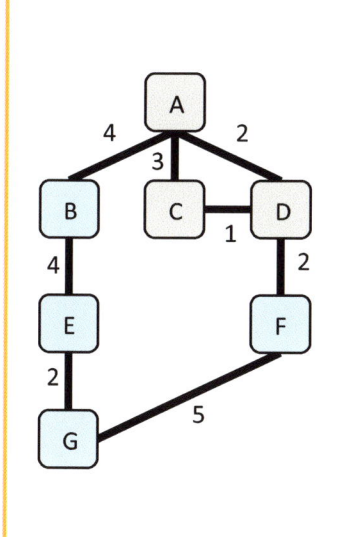

Node	Distance from start	Visited	Previous Node
A	0	Yes	
B	4	No	A
C	3	Yes	A
D	2	Yes	A
E	∞	No	
F	4	No	D
G	∞	No	

Essential algorithms for A level Computer Science

| Step 7 | Select the node with the lowest distance from the start that has not been visited: B. This could also have been F — it doesn't matter which is chosen first. Consider each edge from B that has not been visited: E. |

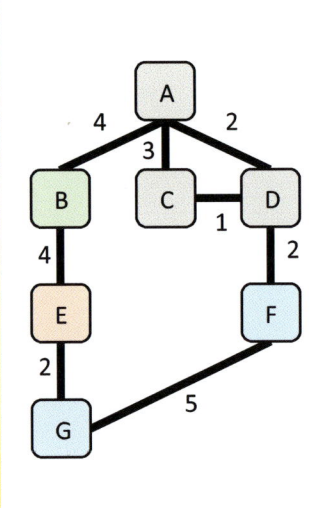

Node	Distance from start	Visited	Previous Node
A	0	Yes	
B	4	No	A
C	3	Yes	A
D	2	Yes	A
E	∞	No	
F	4	No	D
G	∞	No	

| Step 8 | Distance from the start = B's distance from the start + edge weight. E: 4 + 4 = 8 (lower than ∞) – update. Set B to visited. |

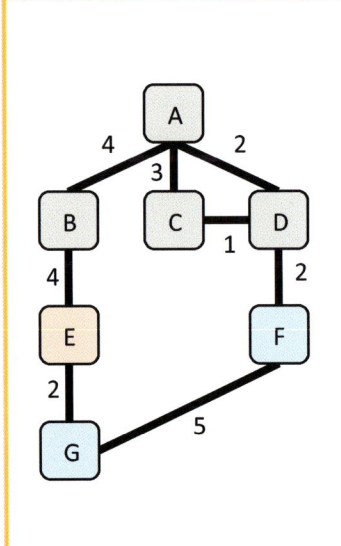

Node	Distance from start	Visited	Previous Node
A	0	Yes	
B	4	Yes	A
C	3	Yes	A
D	2	Yes	A
E	8	No	B
F	4	No	D
G	∞	No	

OPTIMISATION ALGORITHMS

Step 9	Select the node with the lowest distance from the start that has not been visited: F. Consider each edge from F that has not been visited: G.				
		Node	Distance from start	Visited	Previous Node
		A	0	Yes	
		B	4	Yes	A
		C	3	Yes	A
		D	2	Yes	A
		E	8	No	B
		F	4	No	D
		G	∞	No	

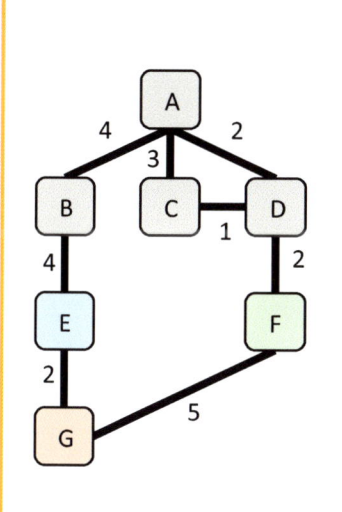

Step 10	Distance from the start = F's distance from the start + edge weight. G: 4 + 5 = 9 (lower than ∞) – update. Set F to visited.				
		Node	Distance from start	Visited	Previous Node
		A	0	Yes	
		B	4	Yes	A
		C	3	Yes	A
		D	2	Yes	A
		E	8	No	B
		F	4	Yes	D
		G	9	No	F

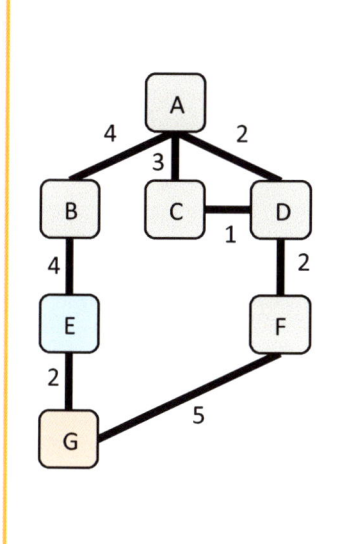

Essential algorithms for A level Computer Science

| Step 11 | Select the node with the lowest distance from the start that has not been visited: E. Consider each edge from F that has not been visited: G. |

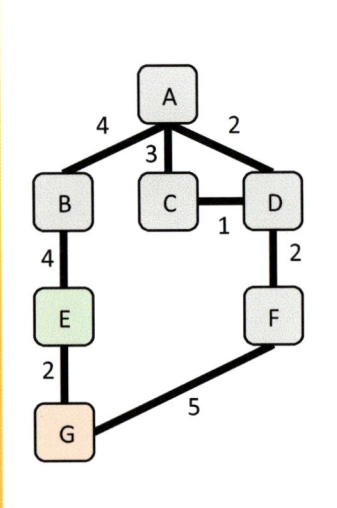

Node	Distance from start	Visited	Previous Node
A	0	Yes	
B	4	Yes	A
C	3	Yes	A
D	2	Yes	A
E	8	No	B
F	4	Yes	D
G	9	No	F

| Step 12 | Distance from the start = E's distance from the start + edge weight. G: 8 + 2 = 10 (not lower than 9) – don't update.). Set E to visited. |

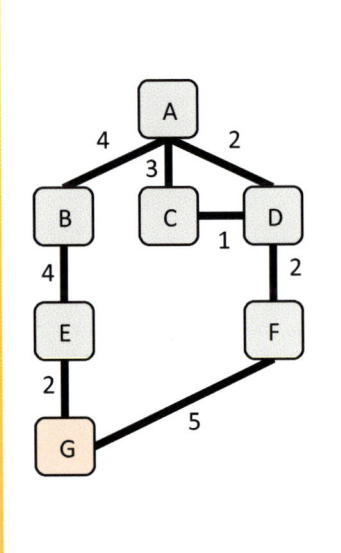

Node	Distance from start	Visited	Previous Node
A	0	Yes	
B	4	Yes	A
C	3	Yes	A
D	2	Yes	A
E	8	Yes	B
F	4	Yes	D
G	9	No	F

Optimisation algorithms

Step 13 — Select the node with the lowest distance from the start that has not been visited: G.
Consider each edge from G that has not been visited: none.

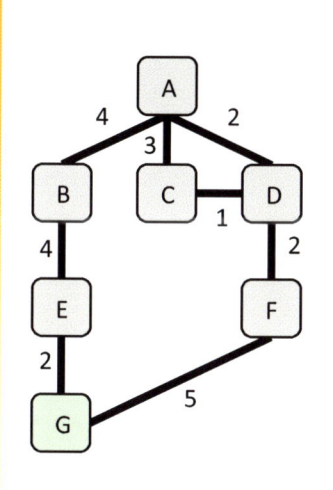

Node	Distance from start	Visited	Previous Node
A	0	Yes	
B	4	Yes	A
C	3	Yes	A
D	2	Yes	A
E	8	Yes	B
F	4	Yes	D
G	9	No	F

Step 14 — No edges to consider.
Set G to visited.

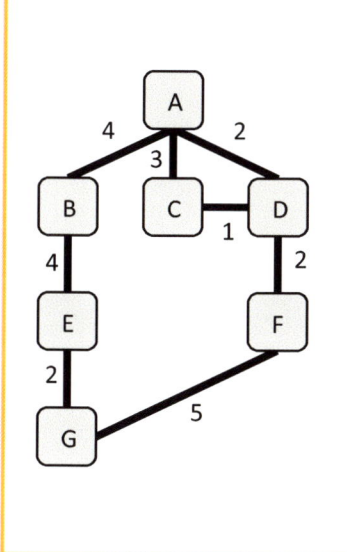

Node	Distance from start	Visited	Previous Node
A	0	Yes	
B	4	Yes	A
C	3	Yes	A
D	2	Yes	A
E	8	Yes	B
F	4	Yes	D
G	9	No	F

Step 15 — There are no unvisited nodes. The algorithm is complete.

To find the shortest path from one node to any other, start with the goal node and follow the previous nodes back to the start, inserting the new node at the front of the list, e.g.:

Shortest path from A to G is: A→D→F→G.

Notice how Dijkstra's algorithm finds the shortest path between all nodes. This is a difference between Dijkstra and the A* algorithm.

Pseudocode for Dijkstra's shortest path

```
Function Dijkstra(graph, start, goal)
    For each vertex in graph
        distance[vertex] = infinity
    Next
    distance[start] = 0
    While unvisited_vertices in graph
        shortest = null
        For each vertex in graph
            If shortest == null Then
                shortest = vertex
            ElseIf distance[vertex] < distance[shortest] Then shortest = vertex
            End If
        Next
        For each neighbour in graph
            If cost + distance[shortest] < distance[neighbour] then
                distance[neighbour] = cost + distance[shortest]
                previous_vertext[neighbour] = shortest
            End If
        Next
        graph.pop(shortest)
    End While
    vertex = goal
    While vertex != start
        shortest_path.insert(vertex)
        vertex = previous_vertex[vertex]
    End While
    Return shortest_path
End Function
```

Did you know?

Adaptations of Dijkstra's shortest path are often the algorithms behind routing protocols in packet switching networks.

Dijkstra's shortest path coded in Python

```python
def dijkstra(graph,start,goal):
    #Initialise
    infinity = float("inf")
    distance = {}
    previous_vertex = {}
    shortest_path = []

    #Set the shortest distance from the start for all vertices to infinity
    for vertex in graph:
        distance[vertex] = infinity
    #Set the shortest distance from the start for the start vertex to 0
    distance[start] = 0

    #Loop until all the vertices have been visited
    while graph:
        #Find the vertex with the shortest distance from the start
        shortest = None
        for vertex in graph:
            if shortest == None:
                shortest = vertex
            elif distance[vertex] < distance[shortest]:
                shortest = vertex

        #Calculate shortest distance for each edge
        for neighbour, cost in graph[shortest].items():
            #Update the shortest distance for the vertex if the new value is lower
            if neighbour in graph and cost + distance[shortest] < distance[neighbour]:
                distance[neighbour] = cost + distance[shortest]
                previous_vertex[neighbour] = shortest

        #The vertex has now been visited, remove it from the vertices to consider
        graph.pop(shortest)

    #Generate the shortest path
    #Start from the goal, adding vertices to the front of the list
    vertex = goal
    while vertex != start:
        shortest_path.insert(0,vertex)
        vertex = previous_vertex[vertex]
    #Add the start vertex
    shortest_path.insert(0,start)

    #Return the shortest shortest_path
    return shortest_path
```

Essential algorithms for A level Computer Science

```python
#Main program starts here
graph = {"A":{"B":4,"C":3,"D":2},"B":{"A":4,"E":4},"C":{"A":3,"D":1},"D":{"A":2,"C":1,"F":2},"E":{"B":4,"G":2},"F":{"D":2,"G":5},"G":{"E":2,"F":5}}
print(dijkstra(graph, "A", "G"))
```

Dijkstra's shortest path coded in Visual Basic Console

```vb
Module Module1
    Function dijkstra(graph As Dictionary(Of String, Dictionary(Of String, Integer)), start As String, goal As String)
        'Initialise
        Dim infinity As Integer = 2147483647
        Dim distance As New Dictionary(Of String, Integer)
        Dim previous_vertex As New Dictionary(Of String, String)
        Dim shortest_path As New List(Of String)
        Dim shortest As String
        Dim cost As Integer

        'Set the shortest distance from the start for all vertices to infinity
        For Each vertex In graph
            distance.Add(vertex.Key, infinity)
        Next
        'Set the shortest distance from the start for the start vertex to 0
        distance(start) = 0

        'Loop until all the vertices have been visited
        While graph.Count > 0
            'Find the vertex with the shortest distance from the start
            shortest = Nothing
            For Each vertex In graph
                If shortest = Nothing Then
                    shortest = vertex.Key
                ElseIf distance(vertex.Key) < distance(shortest) Then
                    shortest = vertex.Key
                End If
            Next

            'Calculate shortest distance for each edge
            For Each neighbour In graph(shortest)
                cost = neighbour.Value
                'Update the shortest distance for the vertex if the new value is lower
                If graph.ContainsKey(neighbour.Key) And cost + distance(shortest) < distance(neighbour.Key) Then
                    distance(neighbour.Key) = cost + distance(shortest)
                    previous_vertex(neighbour.Key) = shortest
                End If
            Next

            'The vertex has now been visited, remove it from the vertices to consider
```

```vbnet
            graph.Remove(shortest)
        End While

        'Generate the shortest path
        'Start from the goal, adding vertices to the front of the list
        Dim current_vertex As String = goal
        While current_vertex <> start
            shortest_path.Insert(0, current_vertex)
            current_vertex = previous_vertex(current_vertex)
        End While
        'Add the start vertex
        shortest_path.Insert(0, start)

        'Return the shortest shortest_path
        Return shortest_path
    End Function

    Sub main()
        Dim graph = New Dictionary(Of String, Dictionary(Of String, Integer)) From {
        {"A", New Dictionary(Of String, Integer) From {{"B", 4}, {"C", 3}, {"D", 2}}},
        {"B", New Dictionary(Of String, Integer) From {{"A", 4}, {"E", 4}}},
        {"C", New Dictionary(Of String, Integer) From {{"A", 3}, {"D", 1}}},
        {"D", New Dictionary(Of String, Integer) From {{"A", 2}, {"C", 1}, {"F", 2}}},
        {"E", New Dictionary(Of String, Integer) From {{"B", 4}, {"G", 2}}},
        {"F", New Dictionary(Of String, Integer) From {{"D", 2}, {"G", 5}}},
        {"G", New Dictionary(Of String, Integer) From {{"E", 2}, {"F", 5}}}
        }

        Dim shortest_path = dijkstra(graph, "A", "G")
        For Each vertex In shortest_path
            Console.WriteLine(vertex)
        Next
        Console.ReadLine()
    End Sub
End Module
```

Essential algorithms for A level Computer Science

Efficiency of Dijkstra's shortest path

Time complexity		
Best case	Average case	Worst case
O(E+V log V) Linearithmic	O(E log V) Linearithmic	O(V^2) Polynomial

A "for" loop is used to set the shortest distance of all the nodes. This part of the algorithm is linear: O(n). The main algorithm makes use of a graph stored as a dictionary, and we assume a time complexity of O(1) for looking up data about each node. A "for" loop is nested in a "while" loop when the shortest distance for each neighbouring vertex is calculated from every connected edge. This means the algorithm has a polynomial complexity at worst — O(V^2) — but different implementations are able to reduce this to O(E log V), where E is the number of edges and V the number of vertices.

Did you know?

Dijkstra's shortest path does not work with negative edge values. The Bellman-Ford algorithm and a further development, Johnson's algorithm, would later provide a solution to this problem.

Dijkstra's shortest path is also an example of a breadth-first search.

Optimisation algorithms

A* pathfinding

The A* pathfinding algorithm is a development of Dijkstra's shortest path. Unlike Dijkstra's algorithm, A* finds the shortest path between two vertices on a weighted graph using heuristics. It performs better than Dijkstra's algorithm because not every vertex is considered. Instead, only the most optimal path is followed to the goal. Known as a best-first search algorithm, with A* pathfinding a heuristic estimates the cost of the path between the next vertex and the goal. It then follows this path. It is important that the heuristic does not over-estimate the cost, thereby choosing an incorrect vertex to move to next. The vertices being considered are referred to as "the fringe". The usefulness of the A* algorithm is determined by the suitability of the heuristic.

About heuristics

In figure 1, in addition to the cost of each edge, you might be able to calculate the distance between a vertex and the goal shown by dotted lines. This additional data, called the heuristic, allows you to determine that B is closer to the goal than C or D. Therefore, B is the vertex that should be followed, even though the cost from A to B is higher than the cost from A to C or D. When determining the shortest path, the cost is added to the heuristic to determine the best path. It is worth noting that the calculation of the heuristic does not need to be mathematically accurate — it just needs to deliver a useful result.

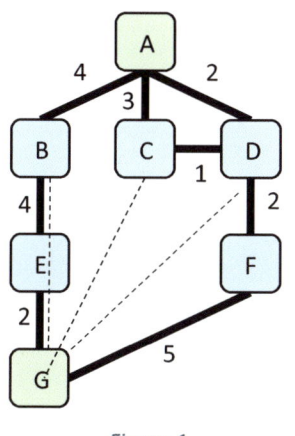

Figure 1

It is easier to appreciate this if we consider a situation in a video game where we want to maximise the frames per second by reducing the number of operations to be performed in a given amount of time. In figure 2, a character at position S (100,20 on the screen) is required to travel to E (80,160) via waypoint B or D. A heuristic measuring the distance between S and E could be calculated using Pythagoras' theorem on the right-angle triangle: $\sqrt{20^2 + 140^2}$ = 141 However, simply adding the two sides (*a* and *o*) requires fewer processing cycles but still delivers a useful result (20 + 140 = 160). We have used the Manhattan distance (the sum of the opposite and adjacent) to estimate C instead of the accurate Euclidian distance (hypotenuse). Estimating results in this way — where only a best guess matters, rather than a precise result — is called a heuristic in computer science.

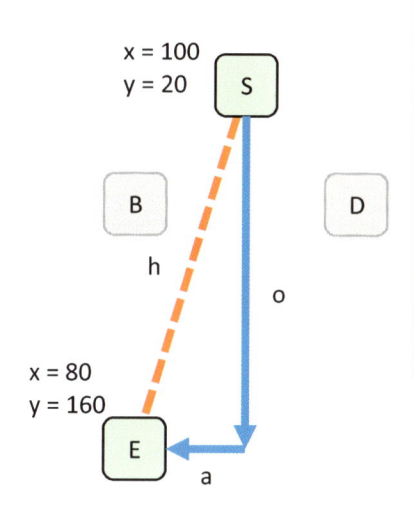

Figure 2

Although the heuristic could potentially be calculated in advance for each vertex, in reality it is only usually calculated for a vertex when needed to maximise the efficiency of the algorithm. In both examples, we used the distance between a start and end-point to determine the heuristic, but this could be any meaningful data relevant to the context. We could make our game character appear more intelligent by changing the heuristic depending on other factors in the game.

The A* algorithm has some notation that programmers of the algorithm will be familiar with:

- The distance from the start of a vertex plus the edge value is often referred to as the 'g' value.

- The distance from the start of a vertex plus the edge value plus the heuristic is often referred to as the 'f' value.

Essential algorithms for A level Computer Science

Exam board clarification

For OCR, candidates do not need to be able to code A* pathfinding. They need to know how it works, calculate the shortest path using the algorithm, and read and trace code that performs the algorithm.

Applications of A* pathfinding

Although useful in travel routing systems, A* is generally outperformed by other algorithms that pre-process the graph to attain a better performance. A* was originally developed as part of the Shakey project to build a robot with artificial intelligence. Frequently found in video games, the algorithm is used to move non-playable characters in a way that they appear move intelligently. It can also be found in network packet routing, in financial modelling for trading assets and goods (arbitrage opportunity), solving puzzles like word ladders, and social networking analysis — calculating degrees of separation between individuals to suggest friends, for example.

Craig'n'Dave video

https://www.craigndave.org/algorithm-astar

A* pathfinding in simple-structured English

To calculate the shortest path:

1. Until the goal node has the lowest *f* value of all the nodes and nodes do not have an *f* value of infinity:
    a. Find the node with the lowest *f* value that has not been visited.
    b. For each connected node that has not been visited:
        i. Calculate the relative distance from the start by adding the edge and the heuristic.
        ii. If the distance from the start plus the heuristic is lower than the currently recorded *f* value:
            1. Set the *f* value of the connected node to the newly calculated distance.
            2. Set the previous node to be the current node.
    c. Set the current node as visited.

To output the shortest path:

2. Start from a goal node
3. Add the previous node to the start of a list.
4. Repeat from step 7 until the start node is reached.
5. Output the list.

A* pathfinding illustrated

If illustrations help you remember, this is how you can picture A* pathfinding:

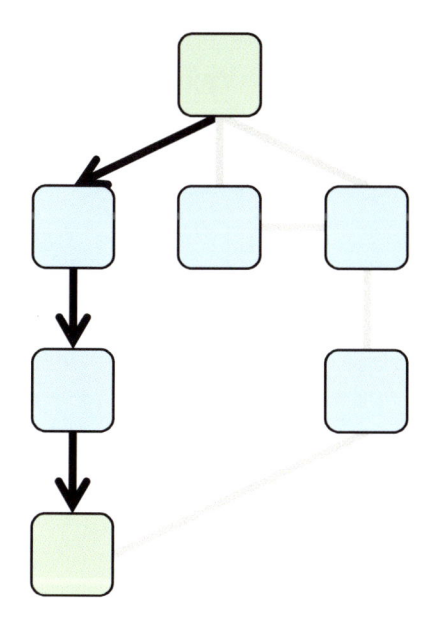

Stepping through A* pathfinding

Note that many authors do not show the starting values for the distance from the start or *f* in their illustrations, but they are infinity for all vertices — except for the start, which has a value of zero. The heuristic for the goal should also be zero.

Step 1	Set the distance from the start to infinity for all nodes. Set the distance from the start to zero for vertex A. Select the node with the lowest *f* value that has not been visited: A. Consider each edge from A that has not been visited: B, C, D.						
	Node	Distance from start	Heuristic	*f*	Visited	Previous Node
	A	0	12	0	No	
	B	∞	6	∞	No	
	C	∞	9	∞	No	
	D	∞	12	∞	No	
	E	∞	3	∞	No	
	F	∞	9	∞	No	
	G	∞	0	∞	No	

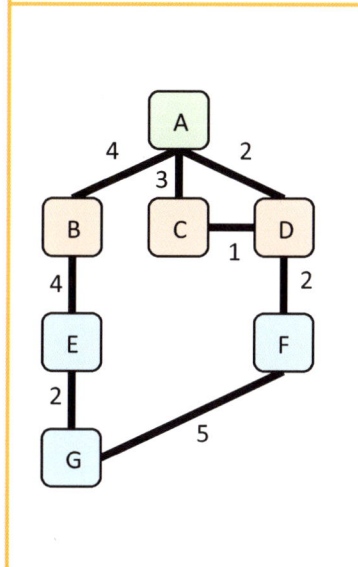

Essential algorithms for A level Computer Science

Step 2

f = A's distance from the start + edge weight + heuristic.
B: 0 + 4 + 6 = 10 (lower than ∞) – update. C: 0 + 3 + 9 = 12 (lower than ∞) – update.
D: 0 + 2 + 12 = 14 (lower than ∞) – update.
Set A to visited.

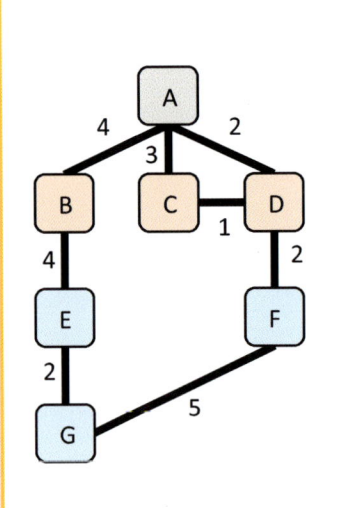

Vertex	Distance from start	Heuristic	f	Visited	Previous Vertex
A	0	12	0	Yes	
B	4	6	10	No	A
C	3	9	12	No	A
D	2	12	14	No	A
E	∞	3	∞	No	
F	∞	9	∞	No	
G	∞	0	∞	No	

Step 3

Select the node with the lowest f value that has not been visited: B.
Consider each edge from B that has not been visited: E.

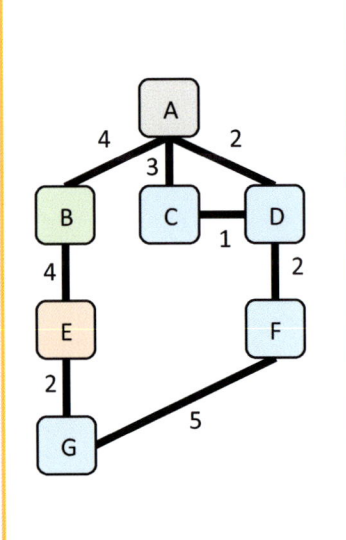

Vertex	Distance from start	Heuristic	f	Visited	Previous Vertex
A	0	12	0	Yes	
B	4	6	10	No	A
C	3	9	12	No	A
D	2	12	14	No	A
E	∞	3	∞	No	
F	∞	9	∞	No	
G	∞	0	∞	No	

Step 4

f = B's distance from the start + edge weight + heuristic.
E: 4 + 4 + 3 = 11 (lower than ∞) – update.
Set B to visited.

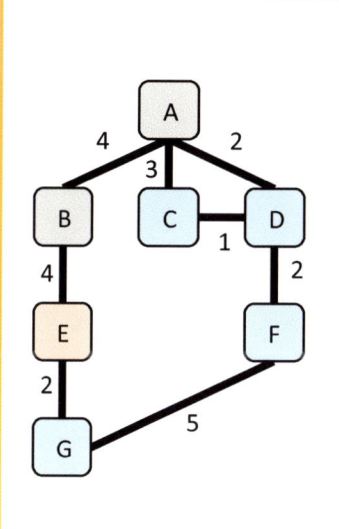

Optimisation algorithms

Node	Distance from start	Heuristic	f	Visited	Previous Node
A	0	12	0	Yes	
B	4	6	10	Yes	A
C	3	9	12	No	A
D	2	12	14	No	A
E	8	3	11	No	B
F	∞	9	∞	No	
G	∞	0	∞	No	

Step 5 — Select the node with the lowest *f* value that has not been visited: E.
Consider each edge from E that has not been visited: G.

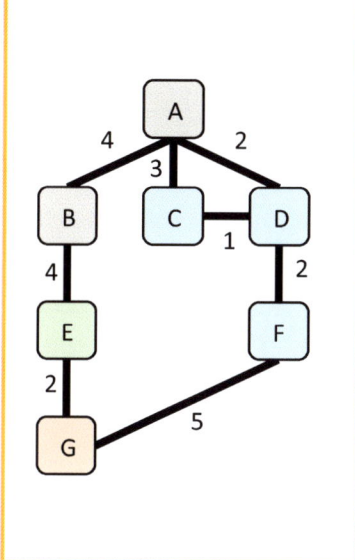

Node	Distance from start	Heuristic	f	Visited	Previous Node
A	0	12	0	Yes	
B	4	6	10	Yes	A
C	3	9	12	No	A
D	2	12	14	No	A
E	8	3	11	No	B
F	∞	9	∞	No	
G	∞	0	∞	No	

Essential algorithms for A level Computer Science

Step 6

f = E's distance from the start + edge weight + heuristic.
G: 8 + 2 + 0 = 10 (lower than ∞) – update.
Set E to visited.

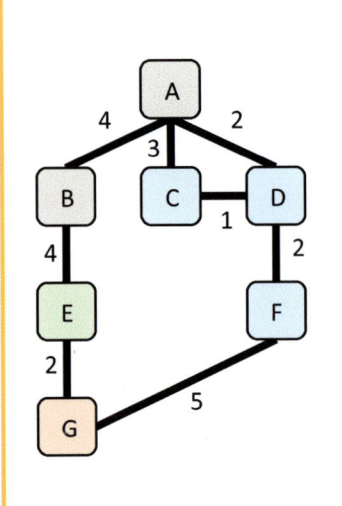

Node	Distance from start	Heuristic	f	Visited	Previous Node
A	0	12	0	Yes	
B	4	6	10	Yes	A
C	3	9	12	No	A
D	2	12	14	No	A
E	8	3	11	Yes	B
F	∞	9	∞	No	
G	10	0	10	No	E

Step 7

Select the node with the lowest *f* value that has not been visited: G.
Consider each edge from G that has not been visited: F.

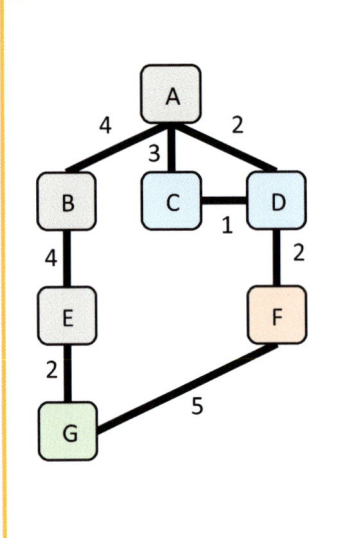

Node	Distance from start	Heuristic	f	Visited	Previous Node
A	0	12	0	Yes	
B	4	6	10	Yes	A
C	3	9	12	No	A
D	2	12	14	No	A
E	8	3	11	Yes	B
F	∞	9	∞	No	
G	10	0	10	No	E

Optimisation algorithms

Step 8	f = G's distance from the start + edge weight + heuristic. F: 10 + 5 + 9 = 24 (lower than ∞) – update. Set G to visited.

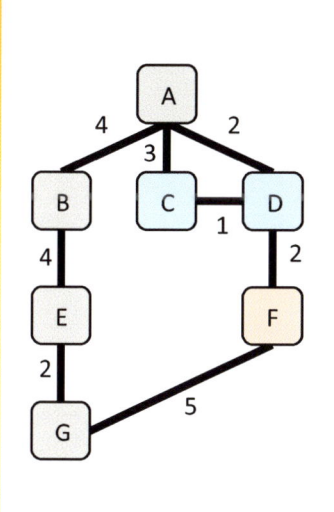

Node	Distance from start	Heuristic	f	Visited	Previous Node
A	0	12	0	Yes	
B	4	6	10	Yes	A
C	3	9	12	No	A
D	2	12	14	No	A
E	8	3	11	Yes	B
F	15	9	24	No	G
G	10	0	10	Yes	E

Step 9	At this point, although vertices C, D and F have not been visited, the goal node G has the lowest value, and no node has an f value of infinity, so the optimal path has been found. The algorithm is complete.

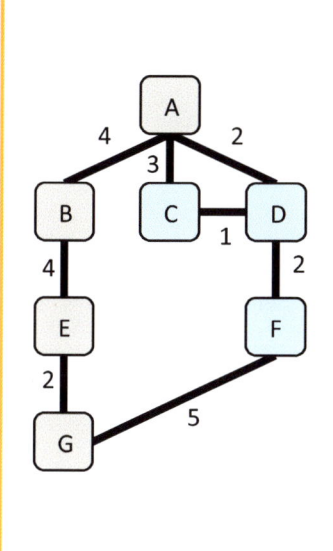

Node	Distance from start	Heuristic	f	Visited	Previous Node
A	0	12	0	Yes	
B	4	6	10	Yes	A
C	3	9	12	No	A
D	2	12	14	No	A
E	8	3	11	Yes	B
F	15	9	24	No	G
G	10	0	10	Yes	E

To find the optimal path, start with the goal node and follow the previous nodes back to the start, inserting the new node at the front of the list, e.g.:

Optimal path from A to G is: A→B→E→G.

Notice how the best path was followed immediately and that it was not necessary to visit C, D or F. This makes A* more efficient that Dijkstra's shortest path because fewer nodes need to be considered. However, A* is only able to find the optimal path between two nodes and not one node to all other nodes. It is also hugely reliant on having a suitable heuristic.

Essential algorithms for A level Computer Science

Pseudocode for A* pathfinding

```
Function Dijkstra(graph, start, goal)
     For each vertex in graph
          distance[vertex] = infinity : f[vertex] = infinity
     Next
     distance[start] = 0 : f[start] = 0
     While unvisited_vertices in graph or f[goal].lowest in graph
          shortest = null
          For each vertex in graph
               If shortest == null Then
                    shortest = vertex
               ElseIf distance[vertex] < distance[shortest] Then shortest = vertex
               End If
          Next
          For each neighbour in graph[shortest]
               If neighbour in graph and cost + distance[shortest] < distance[neighbour]
     then
                    distance[neighbour] = cost + distance[shortest]
                    f[neighbour] = cost + g[shortest] + h[neighbour]
                    previous_vertext[neighbour] = shortest
               End If
          Next
          graph.pop(shortest)
     End While
     vertex = goal
     While vertex != start
          optimal_path.insert(vertex)
          vertex = previous_vertex[vertex]
     End While
     Return optimal_path
End Function
```

Did you know?

The * symbol in computer science is referred to as an asterisk. However, the A* algorithm is called the "A-star algorithm."

A* pathfinding coded in Python

```python
def astar(graph,h,start,goal):
    #Initialise
    infinity = float("inf")
    g = {}
    f = {}
    previous_vertex = {}
    optimal_path = []

    #Set the g and f for all vertices to infinity
    for vertex in graph:
        g[vertex] = infinity
        f[vertex] = infinity
    #Set the g and f from the start vertex to 0
    g[start] = 0
    f[start] = 0

    #Consider each vertex
    while graph:
        #Find the vertex with the shortest f from the start
        shortest = None
        for vertex in graph:
            if shortest == None:
                shortest = vertex
            elif f[vertex] < f[shortest]:
                shortest = vertex

        #Calculate g & f value for each node
        for neighbour, cost in graph[shortest].items():
            #Update f value and previous vertex if lower
            if neighbour in graph and cost + g[shortest] + h[neighbour] < f[neighbour]:
                g[neighbour] = cost + g[shortest]
                f[neighbour] = cost + g[shortest] + h[neighbour]
                previous_vertex[neighbour] = shortest

        #The vertex has now been visited, remove it from the vertices to consider
        graph.pop(shortest)

    #Generate the shortest shortest_path
    #Start from the goal, adding vertices to the front of the list
    vertex = goal
    while vertex != start:
        optimal_path.insert(0,vertex)
        vertex = previous_vertex[vertex]
    #Add the start vertex
    optimal_path.insert(0,start)

    #Return the shortest shortest_path
```

Essential algorithms for A level Computer Science

```python
    return optimal_path

#Main program starts here
graph = {"A":{"B":4,"C":3,"D":2},"B":{"A":4,"E":4},"C":{"A":3,"D":1},"D":{"A":2,"C":1,"F":2},"E":{"B":4,"G":2},"F":{"D":2,"G":5},"G":{"E":2,"F":5}}
h = {"A":12,"B":6,"C":9,"D":12,"E":3,"F":9,"G":0}
print(astar(graph, h, "A", "G"))
```

A* pathfinding coded in Visual Basic Console

```vb
Module Module1
    Function astar(graph As Dictionary(Of String, Dictionary(Of String, Integer)), h As Dictionary(Of String, Integer), start As String, goal As String)
        'Initialise
        Dim infinity As Integer = 2147483647
        Dim g As New Dictionary(Of String, Integer)
        Dim f As New Dictionary(Of String, Integer)
        Dim previous_vertex As New Dictionary(Of String, String)
        Dim shortest_path As New List(Of String)
        Dim shortest As String
        Dim cost As Integer

        'Set the g and f for all vertices to infinity
        For Each vertex In graph
            g.Add(vertex.Key, infinity)
            f.Add(vertex.Key, infinity)
        Next
        'Set the g and f from the start vertex to 0
        g(start) = 0
        f(start) = 0

        'Consider each vertex
        While graph.Count > 0
            'Find the vertex with the shortest f from the start
            shortest = Nothing
            For Each vertex In graph
                If shortest = Nothing Then
                    shortest = vertex.Key
                ElseIf f(vertex.Key) < f(shortest) Then
                    shortest = vertex.Key
                End If
            Next

            'Calculate shortest g & f value for each edge
            For Each neighbour In graph(shortest)
                cost = neighbour.Value
                'Update f value and previous vertex if lower
                If graph.ContainsKey(neighbour.Key) And cost + g(shortest) + h(neighbour.Key) < f(neighbour.Key) Then
```

```vbnet
                    g(neighbour.Key) = cost + g(shortest)
                    f(neighbour.Key) = cost + g(shortest) + h(neighbour.Key)
                    previous_vertex(neighbour.Key) = shortest
                End If
            Next

            'The vertex has now been visited, remove it from the vertices to consider
            graph.Remove(shortest)
        End While

        'Generate the shortest shortest_path
        'Start from the goal, adding vertices to the front of the list
        Dim current_vertex As String = goal
        While current_vertex <> start
            shortest_path.Insert(0, current_vertex)
            current_vertex = previous_vertex(current_vertex)
        End While
        'Add the start vertex
        shortest_path.Insert(0, start)

        'Return the shortest shortest_path
        Return shortest_path
    End Function

    Sub main()
        Dim graph = New Dictionary(Of String, Dictionary(Of String, Integer)) From {
            {"A", New Dictionary(Of String, Integer) From {{"B", 4}, {"C", 3}, {"D", 2}}},
            {"B", New Dictionary(Of String, Integer) From {{"A", 4}, {"E", 4}}},
            {"C", New Dictionary(Of String, Integer) From {{"A", 3}, {"D", 1}}},
            {"D", New Dictionary(Of String, Integer) From {{"A", 2}, {"C", 1}, {"F", 2}}},
            {"E", New Dictionary(Of String, Integer) From {{"B", 4}, {"G", 2}}},
            {"F", New Dictionary(Of String, Integer) From {{"D", 2}, {"G", 5}}},
            {"G", New Dictionary(Of String, Integer) From {{"E", 2}, {"F", 5}}}
        }

        Dim h = New Dictionary(Of String, Integer) From {
            {"A", 12}, {"B", 6}, {"C", 9}, {"D", 12}, {"E", 3}, {"F", 9}, {"G", 0}
        }

        Dim optimal_path = astar(graph, h, "A", "G")
        For Each vertex In optimal_path
            Console.WriteLine(vertex)
        Next
        Console.ReadLine()
    End Sub
End Module
```

Efficiency of A* pathfinding

Time complexity

Best case	Average case	Worst case
$O(b^d)$ Linear	$O(b^d)$ Linear	$O(b^d)$ Polynomial

Determining the efficiency of the A* algorithm is not simple since there are several optimisations that can be implemented and different perspectives on how to calculate the time complexity.

If you study the code carefully, you will see that the algorithm doesn't stop when the goal node has the lowest *f* value but rather, when there are no nodes left to check. The implementation presented is the same as Dijkstra's shortest path, with an added heuristic to determine an optimal path. This is a great example of how a coded solution can exemplify the characteristics of a well-known algorithm while having its own nuance, due to the way it is implemented. This is very common in programming. There are always multiple ways to solve the same problem, some being more efficient than others, in terms of complexity of approach, readability, execution time and memory usage.

Depending on the purpose of A* pathfinding within a larger program, it may only be necessary to compute one path, not necessarily the most optimal path. Therefore, once a solution has been found between the start and the goal, the algorithm can stop. This reduces execution time considerably but would not backtrack to consider other — potentially more optimal — routes.

A common optimisation with A* pathfinding is to pre-calculate the shortest distance or *f* values of some vertices, significantly increasing its efficiency. A simple example of this would be to store the path from A to G in another data structure once it has been calculated. If it is needed again, assuming the heuristic has not changed, instead of being calculated all over again to return the same result, it can simply be looked up.

Having a suitable heuristic that can be calculated quickly is essential. The complexity of this is usually considered to be $O(1)$, although that may not be the case. Where it makes sense to use a Manhattan distance, the heuristic is as optimal as it can be. However, A* is often used in situations where the heuristic is just a computation to deliver a best guess.

Computer science theorists usually consider the execution time of A* as the result of the number of nodes and edges in the graph. However, those working with artificial intelligence consider what is known as the branching factor (b). In AI processing, the number of edges to consider can be extremely large, so an optimisation that avoids having to consider all the nodes would be used. In this case, the number of nodes and edges has less relevance. Therefore, time complexity is more a measurement of the depth to the goal node (d). The time complexity of A* pathfinding is often calculated as polynomial: $O(b^d)$. The values of the branching factor, the goal node and the heuristic affect the efficiency of the algorithm so significantly that it can either be almost linear at best or polynomial at worst.

In summary

Dijkstra's shortest path	A* pathfinding
Finds the shortest path from one node to all other nodes	Finds the shortest path between two nodes
No heuristic	Uses a heuristic
All nodes are expanded during the search	Only promising nodes are expanded during the search
Fails with negative edge values	Fails if the heuristic is over-estimated

ISBN: 978-1-7943594-2-0

Copyright © D.Hillyard and C.Sargent 2018

All rights reserved.

Printed in Great Britain
by Amazon